ROBIN HOOD

Outlaw or Greenwood Myth

Dedication

For all Tonbridge Mummers and Hoodeners — past, present and future

ROBIN HOOD

Outlaw or Greenwood Myth

TEMPUS

First published 2000

PUBLISHED IN THE UNITED KINGDOM BY:
Tempus Publishing Ltd
The Mill, Brimscombe Port
Stroud, Gloucestershire GL5 2QG

PUBLISHED IN THE UNITED STATES OF AMERICA BY:
Tempus Publishing Inc.
2A Cumberland Street
Charleston, SC 29401

Tempus books are available in France, Germany and Belgium
from the following addresses:

Tempus Publishing Group	Tempus Publishing Group	Tempus Publishing Group
21 Avenue de la République	Gustav-Adolf-Straße 3	Place de L'Alma 4/5
37300 Joué-lès-Tours	99084 Erfurt	1200 Brussels
FRANCE	GERMANY	BELGIUM

British Library Cataloguing in Publication Data.
A catalogue record for this book is available from the British Library.

ISBN 0 7524 1479 8

Typesetting and origination by Tempus Publishing.
PRINTED AND BOUND IN GREAT BRITAIN.

Contents

List of Illustrations

Introduction

The concept of an individual who can only find freedom or come to terms with his own true nature by rejecting or withdrawing from his society and entering into an Arcadian or contemplative existence in commune with nature, is an enduring and archetypal European myth extending back at least as far as Timon of Athens. The withdrawal can be a temporary one, as in the case of the Duke in Shakespeare's *As You Like It* or of Prospero in *The Tempest*, who await the restoration of valid values in their societies before returning as rulers. Not only their societies improve, however, but they themselves are the wiser from their experiences in adversity. Writers and film directors who have shown Robin Hood as an aristocrat unjustly deprived of his estates, depict him awaiting a return to play his proper role in society, but with the compassion and wisdom he has learned from his suffering.

Then there are the outlaws such as Hereward the Wake who were banished because of their bad behaviour. In Hereward's case the society which banished him was ruthlessly swept aside by the Norman invasion, but he matured into an heroic freedom fighter (or at least took on that stance in legend), paradoxically trying to reinstate the social order which banished him. Similarly many nineteenth- and twentieth-century American outlaws and Australian bushrangers — figures such as Jessie James, Billy the Kid, Pretty Boy Floyd, Ned Kelly and Ben Hall, committed genuine crimes against their societies, but became folk heroes because they embodied a genuine challenge to some unfair aspect within the operations of society and its authority (often as in the Robin Hood legends embodied in the authority of local sheriffs). As Woody Guthrie sang in his ballad *Pretty Boy Floyd*: 'some rob you with a six gun, some with a fountain pen' and

> As through this world you travel, as through this world you roam,
> you'll never see an outlaw, drive a family from their home.

The context here is the dustbowl eviction of farmers from mid-west America in the thirties, when banks ruthlessly foreclosed on the mortgages of bankrupt farmers and evicted them and their families. Petty Boy Floyd shares with Robin Hood the tradition of stealing from the rich and giving to the poor and the dislike of sheriffs, whose power they regard as arbitrary, and associated with vested interest.

What about the concept of the outlaw as freedom fighter? William Tell immediately springs to mind, and numerous nineteenth- and twentieth-century fighters against oppressive regimes. Ever since Joseph Ritson, himself a supporter of the French Revolution, wrote his biography of Robin Hood in 1795, which influenced Scott's *Ivanhoe*, children's writers and films have shown Robin championing the poor against the rich and specifically the Saxon peasantry against their Norman overlords with their feudal system and savage game laws. To what extent did the late twelfth-century and thirteenth-century peasants consider themselves as Anglo-Saxons unfairly treated by Norman oppressors? Or was it the simply the usual case of the rich exploiting the poor? These are interesting questions as the Anglo-Saxon aristocracy undoubtedly treated their peasantry better than the Normans did — they didn't have to build castles to protect themselves against their own people. The Hereward revolt was definitely one of Anglo-Saxons (aided at times by Vikings) against the Normans.

How does Robin Hood fit into this outlaw tradition? In the late nineteenth century, the great ballad scholar Francis Child regarded Robin as 'absolutely a creation of the ballad-muse'. How wonderful was the absolute certainty of those nineteenth-century scholars! Yet few would agree with Professor Child's conclusion today, though his ballad scholarship remains unequalled and of enormous value to all researchers into Robin Hood. In the twentieth century there has been scholarly pursuit of Robin as an historical outlaw and as a figure from the May Games.

Ever since Ritson's book there has been a strong interest in trying to prove and locate an historical Robin Hood with links with Barnsdale or Sherwood Forest or both. Professor Holt's *Robin Hood* is the definitive work in the historical approach to the Robin Hood legend, examining candidates and exploring the concept of 'yeoman' and the social, economic, political, religious and geographical background with great thoroughness and clarity. David Wiles and more recently Ronald Hutton have examined the strong role of Robin in the May Games. And Professor R.B. Dobson and J. Taylor have made accessible ballads, literary extracts, play texts and legendary sites in their *Rimes of Robin Hood*, which also contains an excellent introductory essay.

Yet amid all this burgeoning scholarship, the legend was beginning to lose its grassroots appeal in the early 1980s. The problem was that the stories had become too 'Boys' Ownish' through generations of children's books, and films and television series largely made for children. Ever since the publication of *Ivanhoe* the Robin Hood legends had been transmitted largely through children's books, and latterly films. The exception to this were the orally transmitted folksongs being collected up until at least the Aberdeenshire farmer John Strachan's *Robin Hood and Little John* in the 1950s. We have come across many of these ballads being sung in folk clubs since the folk revival of the 1960s, so once again they have an oral currency.

By the early 1980s, interest among the general public in the Robin Hood legends was distinctly on the wane. By comparison with Arthurian tradition, the Robin Hood legends lacked coherence, romance, the supernatural and the mystical, intricate stories and the subtlety of characterisation. Above all it lacked the interest of leading literary writers through the ages — there were no outstanding authors on Robin Hood to compare with Geoffrey of Monmouth, Chretien De Troyes, Malory or Tennyson.

A dramatic change was effected by Richard Carpenter's *Robin of Sherwood* TV series, which awakened a whole new generation's interest in Robin Hood by vigorous characterisation (a marvellously evil Sheriff and a sidekick for him — Guy of Gisborne), realistically earthy outlaws with vitality and humour, by a creative use of the traditional stories and most of all by the introduction — or should we say reintroduction? — of myth, that most powerful ingredient of Arthurian legends. Within months the dying Robin Hood legends were saved, theme parks began to open and shops were full of Robin Hood books once again and videos. Carpenter respected the tradition (he corresponded with a friend of ours about the Guy of Gisborne tradition) but he also provided a series that was somehow both more medieval and more modern than the preceding children's books and films.

Richard Carpenter had, because so little of the original myth of Robin Hood had survived, ingeniously wedded another forest legend — that of Herne the Hunter — with the Robin Hood tradition. This gave both a structure and a whole new dimension to the stories, in the same way rather as the immortality of Arthur, the 'once and future king' with his associations with Avalon affected the Arthurian legends. Did the original Robin Hood legends have a supernatural aspect?

The complexity of recent finds of early surnames 'Robynhode' suggests to us that it is no longer realistic to expect to find a single historical personage who spawned the legends. We feel that it is time to review the whole corpus of the legends and their cultural significance in the light of the recent research, to investigate the possibility of a mythical and folklore origin for Robin, which could have interacted with actual historical people during the development of the legends. In this way the deep subconscious attractions the legends continue to exert might be better understood.

It is hoped that the extensively researched gazetteer of Robin Hood sites (many of which we have visited and photographed) will assist those of you who enjoy outdoor research. As films are now a major source of culture for the young, three members of the younger generation — Isobel Doel, Steven Morley and Thomas Doel — have compiled a filmography of Robin Hood films and television serials as an appendix to the book.

1 The Robin Hood ballads and the outlaw tradition

Herkens, god yemen,
Comley, corteys and god,
On of the best that yeuer bare bowe,
Hes name was Roben Hode
(Robin Hood & the Potter)

Most of what we know about the alleged exploits of Robin Hood comes from a lengthy medieval poem and an assortment of ballads of varying dates; plus three plays (two of them fragmentary) from the May Games overlapping with material in the ballads. It is therefore hardly surprising that Professor Francis Child, the famous nineteenth-century American ballad scholar from Harvard University, was of the opinion that 'Robin Hood is absolutely a creation of the ballad-muse'. We do not necessarily agree with Professor Child's conclusion, but an investigation of the ballads to see the nature of the legend we are dealing with is a sensible starting point, before embarking on the quest for historical and/or mythological origins of our Greenwood hero.

Professor Child's own *English and Scottish Popular Ballads* remains the definitive collection. A lengthy poem (the *Gest*), Martin Parker's *A True Tale of Robin Hood* (an antiquarian rewrite of 1632) and thirty-six ballads (some printed with alternative versions) are printed in Volume Three. A further ballad, found under the title of *The Birth of Robin Hood* in Jamieson's *Popular Ballads* and Buchan's *Ballads of the North of Scotland* is printed in Child's second volume under the title *Willie and Earl Richard's Daughter*. The *Gest*, extracts from Parker and a selection of fourteen Child ballads are reprinted in the excellent modern compendium of Robin Hood literature *Rymes of Robin Hood* by Professor Richard Dobson & John Taylor. There are also a number of Robin Hood ballads of uncertain date and pedigree which did not find their way into Professor Child's collection, An example is the Derbyshire ballad *The Lay of the Buckstone* which seems to have been

I.—A LYTELL GESTE OF ROBYN HODE.

1   *A Lytell Geste of Robyn Hode* — *engraving after Bewick from Joseph Ritson*, Robin Hood

arranged in the nineteenth century from two distinct earlier ballads involving a fight between Robin Hood and the keepers of Peak Forest, and an archery contest between Robin and the Peak Foresters. Another is *Robin Whood (sic) Turned Hermit* published by a Lincolnshire antiquarian in 1735.

Despite recent theories about the chanting of ballads, we are convinced that most of the Robin Hood ballads were either composed as songs or were subsequently provided with tunes. There is considerable evidence that ballads generally and Robin Hood ballads specifically were sung. Jamieson collected *The Birth of Robin Hood* from Mrs Brown of Falkirk, a singer known to Sir Walter Scott and Christie printed the ballad in his *Traditional Ballad Airs* and commented that it was sung by his maternal grandfather. In Kinloch's version there is a reference in the text to 'mony ane sings o Robin Hood'. A number of printed versions of Robin Hood ballad texts are accompanied by instructions as to which tunes they should be sung to and some of the Robin Hood ballads seem to have shared tunes.

Professor Bronson's *The Singing Tradition of Child's Popular Ballads* prints tunes for eight Robin Hood Ballads. The tunes for *Robin Hood's Death* and *The Rescue of Will Stutly* (Child's *Robin Hood Rescuing Will*

A True Tale of *ROBIN HOOD*.

Or, A Brief Touch of the Life and Death of that renowned Outlaw *Robert* Earl of *Huntington*, vulgar-
ly called *Robin Hood*, who lived and dyed in A.D.
1198. being the 9th. year of the Reign of King
Richard the First, commonly called *Richard Cœur
de Lyon*.

Carefully collected out of the truest Writers of our
English Chronicles : And published for the satisfa-
ction of those who desire truth from falshood.

By *Martin Parker.*

Printed for *J. Clark, W. Thackeray*, and
near *West-Smithfield*. 1687.

2 *Frontispiece to Clark & Thackeray's 1687 edition of Martin Parker's* A
True Tale of Robin Hood

Stutly) were supplied in America in 1913 by Martha Davis from her grandmother and reach back through three generations of a family from Virginia back through Maryland to a Pennsylvania settlement of Scotch-Irish. The family used an almost identical tune to the Will Stutly one for their *Robin Hood and Allen a Dale* ballad. Tunes for *Robin Hood's Progress to Nottingham* have been recovered in the nineteenth century from Nova Scotia (Bronson prints one from Devil's Island).

Robin Hood and Little John (recorded by the School of Scottish Studies as sung by the Aberdeen farmer John Strachan); *Robin Hood and the Tanner* (sung and recorded by the contemporary Nottingham folksinger Roy Harris and many others); *Robin Hood and The Pedlar* (Child's *The Bold Pedlar and Robin Hood* sung by the Horsham traditional singer Henry Burstow and collected by Lucy Broadwood); *Robin Hood Rescuing Three Squires* (collected by Percy Grainger and Vaughan Williams) and *Robin Hood and the Bishop of Hereford* (collected by Gardiner and Hammond from Hampshire and Dorset respectively) survive extensively in the oral tradition in England (and in some cases Scotland). Hammond's *Robin Hood and the Bishop of Hereford* was collected from George Stone of Wareham, Dorset in 1906 and he had learned it nearly sixty years before. We ourselves have run a traditional folksong club in Kent for twenty years and have heard a number of Robin Hood ballads performed there.

On the question of ballads and tunes Professor Bronson has commented:

> the tune is a potent aide-memoire. There are numberless instances of ballads in fragmentary state, where the narrative is so confused, disordered even in its central incidents, or all but forgotten, that everything would have been lost, were it not for the tune ... Narrative interest, then, is not essential for survival, and still less suspense or climax. But a tune is essential.
>
> (Bronson, *The Singing Tradition of Child's Popular Ballads*, Introduction, p xxv)

The most important source for Robin Hood's activities, however, is the mediaeval poem *A Gest of Robyn Hode*. This is probably derived from several ballads and uses the traditional ballad metre of four lines rhyming ABAB, with alternate four and three stressed lines, but was probably composed to be read (like the mediaeval romances) rather than to be sung. No manuscript survives for the *Gest*, but it was printed many times in the sixteenth and seventeenth centuries. The

3   Robin Hood, William Scadlock and Little John from the broadside Robin Hood and the Prince of Aragon *(c 1660)*

earliest edition is probably the Lettersnijder version (possibly printed in Antwerp between 1510 and 1515) and this was used by Professor Child as his basic text. However it was incomplete and Child supplemented it from Wynken de Worde's printed version (dated somewhere between 1492 and 1534) to give 456 four-line stanzas. Professor Child felt that some of the linguistic forms in the *Gest* might date it back to 1400 in manuscript form. The individual stories within the *Gest* could well be even earlier and some are paralleled by surviving early Robin Hood ballads.

'Gest' is from *gesta*, the Latin for 'story' and the cycle, consisting of eight stories or 'fitts', is put together with some sophistication with themes such as Robin's devotion to the Virgin Mary ('Our dere Lady,/That he loued allther moste') and a parodying of the epic and romance genres, with Robin as a self-assured yeoman, who parodies the chivalric gestures and courtesy ('So curtesyse an outlawe./Was never non founde') of upper class outlaw heroes of romances such as Fulk Fitzwarin, Hereward the Wake, Eustace the Monk and Gameleyn whose

4   Robin Hood & the Princess from Robin Hood & the Prince of Aragon. *Engraving after Bewick from Ritson's* Robin Hood

genres, deeds and attitudes have been shown as influences on the Gest in Maurice Keen's book *The Outlaws of Medieval England*. Robin's courtesy is praised in the way that Gawain's is in Arthurian tradition, but Robin's courteous treatment of women has a religious impetus:

> Robyn loued Oure dere Lady;
> For dout of dydly synne,
> Wolde he neuer do compani harme
> That any woman was in.

The likely origin of the Gest is that a skilled writer has put together a Robin Hood epic (as Malory, or at least Caxton in his reworking and printing of Malory's romances, did for King Arthur) from a number of traditional stories and ballads.

Robin's chief habitat in the Gest is Barnsdale, in Yorkshire, an area of about twenty five square miles, well wooded in parts, straddling Watling Street from the outskirts of Doncaster to the River Went. The large number of specific local place-names in the Gest do seem to point to the remembered activities of a specific outlaw or outlaw band. Wynkyn de Worde's edition stresses the importance of the sheriff in its title — 'Here begynneth a lytell geste of Robyn Hode and his meyne, And of the proude sheryfe of Notyngham'. Inevitably then, Nottingham features as well (though Sherwood Forest (some forty miles south of Barnsdale and across the county boundary in Nottinghamshire) is not specifically mentioned) and the impression is that the Gest combines stories from the two locations.

In Fitt One, Robin and his followers await an adventure in Barnsdale so that Robin can dine. This borrows an Arthurian convention as in many mediaeval Arthurian romances (eg *Sir Gawain and the Green Knight*). Arthur will not dine until he has experienced an adventure. There is a practical side in Robin's case as he wishes to entertain a guest to dinner from whom he can later require payment for hospitality. Robin instructs his followers (Little John, Much the Miller's Son and Will Scarlok) not to harm knights, squires or yeomen and identifies his traditional enemies:

> These bisshopes and these archebishoppes;
> Ye shall them bete and bynde;
> The hye sheriff of Notyingham
> Hym holden ye in your mynde.

Robin captures an impoverished knight, Sir Richard at Lee, wines and dines him sumptuously and asks him to pay up. On learning that he has mortgaged his lands to the Abbot of St Mary's Abbey, York, for £400 to save the life of his son (who has slain an adversary in a tournament), Robin lends Sir Richard £400 to repay his debt and save his lands. In Fitt Two Sir Richard repays the unpleasant Abbot of St Mary's and his cronies, who are disappointed not to be able to get their hands on his lands.

In Fitt Three Little John enters the Sheriff of Nottingham's employment in disguise and decamps with the Sheriff's cook (after an epic fight) and plate to the Greenwood. They decoy the Sheriff into the forest and capture him and force him to dine off his own dinner service and to sleep rough:

> This is harder order, sayde the sherief
> Than any ankir or frere.

The sheriff is released on giving his word not to persecute the outlaws.

In Fitt Four, Robin captures the High Celarer (Treasurer) of St Mary's Abbey York, as he rides through Barnsdale. In a structure paralleling, yet subtly differing from, Fitt One, the Celarer is captured, wined and dined and asked to pay for his entertainment. Whereas Sir Richard praised the reputation of Robin Hood in Fitt One ('He is a gode yoman ... /Of hym I haue herde moche gode.'), the Monk is critical ('He is a stronge thefe./Of hym herd I neuer good.'). Like Sir Richard, the Monk claims to have no money, but in this case he is found to have £800. In a highly comic scene the outlaws claim that this money cannot be his since he has denied having any. Little John suggests that the Virgin Mary, to whom the Celarer's Abbey is dedicated, is repaying Sir Richard's debt to Robin twofold: 'Our Lady hath doubled your cast.' — an amusing almost blasphemous gambling metaphor. There is a special relationship between the Virgin and Robin in the ballads. The Celarer is released unharmed, but the outlaws keep the money, and decline Sir Richard's proffered return of his loan and instead give him an extra £400. The author of the *Geste* does all he can to generate sympathy for the outlaws, by showing their kind help to a distressed knight, and by showing the Abbey to be involved in extortion and its Celarer to be a churlish liar. The Statute of Mortmain of 1279 forbade Abbeys to lend money at interest or for speculation, so that part of the story may have originated before that date.

Fitt Five describes the famous incident in Robin Hood lore of the archery tournament at Nottingham for the prize of a gold and silver arrow. Little John, Will, Much, and another of Robin's outlaw band, Gilbert of the White Hand, shoot excellently, but Robin wins the prize, which leads to his near capture by the Sheriff. Sir Richard at Lee gives the outlaws shelter in his Castle.

Fitt Six shows how the Sheriff captures Sir Richard in revenge, binds him and imprisons him in Nottingham Castle. Sir Richard's Lady enters the Greenwood to seek help from Robin and the outlaws free Sir Richard. A darker motif is introduced into this section with the killing of the Sheriff by Robin. Generally the early Robin Hood ballads can be divided into categories of violent and non-violent/comic; the fact that the Gest mixes the genres is further indication that its sources are a number of distinct early ballads (some of which survive in slightly later form). The poet tries to justify the killing of the Sheriff by his harsh treatment of Sir Richard and by the fact that he has broken his word by trying to bring the outlaws to justice:

> Lye thou there, thou proude sherife,
> Evyll mote thow cheve!   (evil befall thee)
> There myght no man to the truste   (no man might trust thee)
> The whyles thou were a lyve.

5   *Robin Hood and the Tanner — after an engraving from Bewick in Ritson's* Robin Hood *(1795)*

In Fitt Seven, King Edward, hearing of the death of his sheriff, comes in disguise as an abbot to Sherwood and is captured and wined and dined by the outlaws as with his predecessors in the Gest. After dinner Robin and his men indulge in archery practice, with Robin giving a buffet to anyone missing the target. Eventually Robin misses the target himself and is given a buffet by the abbot that knocks him down. He immediately recognises the King by the strength of his arm and asks pardon for himself and his followers and they all enter the King's service. Because of the dating of the legends, the King's mighty blow and his disguise, it is possible that the King in question was originally intended to have been Richard the Lionheart.

In Fitt Eight, the King decides to play a trick on the people of Nottingham and dresses himself and his men in Lincoln Green as outlaws and marches on the town. The depiction of the terrified townspeople fleeing, even the sick and infirm, is at odds with Robin's supposed local popularity. Robin spends all his money in the King's service and after about eighteen months returns with Little John and Will to Barnsdale, where they live for another twenty two years, before Robin falls sick. He visits his kinswoman, the Prioress at Kirklees

Abbey, who with her lover Roger of Doncaster (a further attack on the double standards of the medieval Roman Catholic Church) plots Robin's death by pretending to cure him by bleeding him, but taking excessive blood.

In the very last line of the poem comes the first reference to Robin's traditional help of the poor:

> ..he was a good outlawe,
> And dyde pore men moch god.

A number of early texts of ballads survive, two of which were saved by Bishop Percy from a seventeenth-century manuscript being used for a fire in a Shrophire farmhouse. One of these texts, *Robin Hood and Guy of Gisborne*, was printed by Percy in his famous *Reliques of Ancient English Poetry* in 1765, an important influence on the Romantic Movement and on the young Sir Walter Scott. The Gisborne story is paralleled by an early play fragment of c1475 and the linguistic form of the ballad suggests a similar date in origin or a few years later.

The ballad begins with a dream, a medieval poetic convention, a premonition of evil. Robin quarrels with Little John, who is subsequently captured by the Sheriff. Sir Guy is a bounty hunter after Robin Hood, whom he does not recognise on first meeting. After a shooting match Robin reveals his identity and they fight to the death, Robin killing Sir Guy. Robin disguises himself as Sir Guy and disfigures the dead Sir Guy's face so that he cannot be recognised. He fools the Sheriff into allowing him to dispatch Little John, whom he frees. John kills the fleeing Sheriff with an arrow.

This is a savage and violent ballad and, again, as in the *Gest*, the Sheriff is killed, this time by Little John. There is evidence that Sir Guy featured is a number of ballads in his own right and William Dunbar includes him in a list of outlaws including Robin Hood in his poem *Epetaphe for Donald Owre*:

> Was never wyld Robein under bewch,
> Nor yet Roger off Clekniskleuch,
> So baud a berne as he;
> Gy off Gysburne, na Allan Bell,
> Na Simonis sonnes off Quhynfell,
> At schot war never so slie.

In recent years Richard Carpenter has revitalised him as the Sheriff's scapegoat and accident-prone sidekick in the television series *Robin of*

6   *Little John knocks Robin into the river. From Howard Pyle's* The Merry Adventures of Robin Hood of Great Renown *(New York, 1883)*

7   *Illustration from the broadside* Robin Hood and the Bishop *(Roxburghe Ballads c 1660)*

Sherwood, possibly borrowing the idea from the 1938 Erroll Flynn film *The Adventures of Robin Hood*.

The other Robin Hood ballad in the manuscript (known as *The Percy Folio*) is *Robin Hoode his Death* which deals with the same subject matter as the end of the *Gest* and has been tentatively dated to about 1500. It is the only Robin Hood ballad which has a haunting, fatalistic, even ritualistic aura, with a touch of the supernatural or of the fates with the old woman 'banning' Robin Hood as he crosses the 'blacke water'. The manuscript is damaged at the point where Robin questions the old woman as to why she is banning Robin Hood, but part of her answer is that:

> Wee weepen for his deare body,
> That this day must be lett bloode.

The word 'bann' and the weeping old woman seem to be in the context of the 'banshee' tradition, defined by *Chambers Dictionary* as: 'A female fairy in Ireland and elsewhere who wails and shrieks before a death in the family to which she is attached.'

This is the one surviving scene in a Robin Hood ballad which clearly gives a strong atmosphere of ritual, mythology and fatalism and which hints at another possible dimension to the significance of the Robin Hood legend.

This ballad differs from the *Gest* in having Robin restrain Little John from revenge on the Abbey of Kirklees, An eighteenth-century version, *The English Archer* is the first to record the scene subsequently immortalised in children's editions and illustrations, of the dying Robin firing an arrow through the Abbey window to site his grave.

The earliest surviving Robin Hood ballad is probably *The Talkyng of the Munke and Robyn Hode* (Robin Hood and the Monk), dateable to about 1450. In this ballad Robin and Little John quarrel over a shooting competition, part company and Robin is captured whilst attending mass in church. John rescues him and is offered the leadership of the band by Robin — which he declines. This is another violent ballad in which Much the Miller's Son kills a little pageboy to silence him.

Robin Hood & the Potter (c 1500), by contrast is a comic ballad, in which both Robin and the Sheriff are in turn discomforted, but the sheriff is allowed to return unharmed to his 'ffoll godde' wife, picking up the reference to Robin's courtesy at the beginning of the ballad:

Ffor the loffe of owre ladey,
All wemen werschepped he.

Robin is defeated in a fight by a Potter and then changes clothes with him, sells pots to the Sheriff's wife and decoys the Sheriff to the Greenwood, where he is robbed, but released unharmed for his wife's sake. This story also survives in a sixteenth-century May Games play. An earlier story concerning the outlaw and freedom fighter Hereward the Wake, has him disguising as a potter to learn the military plans of the Normans.

About a further thirty distinct ballads survive (many in multiple versions) from the seventeenth-, eighteenth- and nineteenth-century broadsides and chapbooks and from the oral tradition in England and America. A large number of these later ballads have a consistent pattern — that of Robin being worsted in quarterstaff fights by a wide range of people such as Little John, Friar Tuck and Arthur A' Bland the Tanner, a Ranger, and a Scotsman, many of whom subsequently join Robin's outlaw band. In one ballad Robin is even defeated By Maid Marian in disguise. *Robin Hood & the Bishop* and *Robin Hood & the Bishop of Hereford* show Robin robbing rich prelates. In the second of these Robin ironically shows more charity than the prelate, who was going to hand Robin over to justice when he thinks he has captured him (Robin is acting as a decoy). There are a number of ballads about Robin rescuing members of the outlaw band, to show its power of comitatus.

One of the keenest debates in Robin Hood scholarship is whether the Robin Hood of the ballads predates the Robin Hood of the May Games. In the next three chapters we shall turn our attention to the latter and its antecedents.

2 The Pastourelles

j'ai ami, bel et cointe et gai.
(Marion's speech from *Li Gieus de Robin et de Marion*)

The pastourelles had grown out of the archaic pastoral, a genre of great antiquity which traditionally took as its subject matter the life of the shepherd, though it embraced other rustic groupings such as fishermen, goatherds, cowherds etc. The earliest 'pastoral' poet is considered to be the third-century BC Greek poet, Theocritus of Syracuse in Sicily, (316-260BC), who in his 'entertainments', poetic dialogues and monologues, established the prototype of the pastoral — a romanticised and nostalgic presentation of the shepherds' life as innocent of the corrupting influences of the court and whose characters invariably displayed naive but engaging qualities. The subject matter of the poetry involved contest (either in piping or song improvisation) and heterosexual love interest either in a eulogy or discussion of the attractions of young country women. The poetry of Theocritus was written to be delivered before a very particular and sophisticated audience, wealthy Greeks living in Alexandria, and is likely to have had accompanying professional musicians to enhance the performance.

The genre was to re-emerge and become very popular in thirteenth-century Europe particularly in Germany, Italy and France.

One pastourelle is notable in that it influenced the English pastourelle used in the May Games. It was written by Adam de la Halle, a poet and musician from Arras round about the year 1280 while he was working as a court poet. De la Halle's play, *Li Gieues de Robin et de Marion* (The Game of Robin and Marion) is written in a northern French dialect and in poetic form, using the then popular octosyllabic couplet. De la Halle provided a considerable amount of lively folk-type music for the play (still extant) and it seems from the text that there was accompanied and unaccompanied singing as well as some energetic dancing with musicians playing cornetts, and possibly bagpipes and a drum.

The text itself indicates the costuming of the play which for the shepherds and shepherdesses and knight are contemporary with the date of writing, that is late thirteenth century. The knight is in hunting gear with a falconer's gauntlet. The shepherds are not in their workday smocks but in belted coats and leggings and carry leather 'scrips', a kind of satchel in which food can be stored. Marion and Peronelle, the heroine and her special friend (the parts may have been played by young boys with unbroken voices) wear long dresses with belts over petticoats and in one scene have cloaks. Peronelle wears a straw hat and Marion a simple and traditional garland of flowers in her loose hair. Both their bodices appear to be voluminous (it is possible that for country women this type of loose, cross-over bodice enabled them to feed babies easily). Not being mothers, Marion and Peronelle pragmatically use the space as pockets in which objects might be carried — bread and cheese in the case of Marion — and Peronelle has stored a number of items in her bodice, which, because it looks lumpy, occasions a great deal of amusement.

Props mentioned and used in the text include a crook and a knife, a basket and an earthenware or leather water pitcher, while Robin's friends carry shillelaghs and a pitchfork. Real lambs may have been used in performance and are mentioned in the text but the knight's falcon may have been stuffed as Robin is supposed to maul it and enrage its owner. The knight, as is fitting, is mounted, though a hobby-horse is likely to have been employed. Marion is to be abducted and carried off on horseback protesting raucously.

The play could have been staged equally well indoors or outdoors as all that is required in the way of scenery is a bush behind which Robin and his friends spy on the lascivious knight, and a grassy mound used when the rustic company play an unseasonal Christmas game that would permit bawdy extempore gestures and actions.

De la Halle's *Le Gieus de Robin et de Marion* uses what is possibly the best known pastourelle theme: the near seduction of a young shepherdess by a knight. A sophisticated court of the period would have been aware of the seminal work *The Art of Courtly Love* (De Arte Honeste Amandi) by Andreas Capellanus chaplain to Marie, Duchesse de Champagne and written some years before but still popular in court circles. The work professed to be a handbook for courtly lovers but was in fact an outrageously funny spoof of *Ars Amatoria* (The Art of Loving) by the first-century BC Roman poet Ovid. In *The Art of Courtly Love* Capellanus gives knights some tongue-in-cheek good advice in a section entitled 'On The Love of Peasants':

BOOK III.

"Lusty Robin Hood, who long time like a king
Within her compass lived, and when he list to range
For some rich booty set, or else his air to change,
To Sherwood still retired.
        *   *   *
In this our spacious isle, I think there is not one,
But he hath heard some talk of him and Little John
And to the end of time the tales shall ne'er be done,
Of Scarlock, George-a-Green, and Much, the miller's son
Of Tuck the merry friar."   DRAYTON.

8   *Robin Hood teaches Marian how to shoot. From Pierce Egan's* Robin Hood & Little John *(1840)*

If you should, by some chance, fall in love with a peasant girl, take care to puff her up with lots of praise, and then, when you find a suitable spot, do not delay in taking what you want and embrace her by force. This is because you can hardly soften their outward inflexibility so far that they will permit you to embrace them without a struggle or allow you to have the relief you so desire unless first you use a little compulsion as a convenient cure for their timidity. We do not say these things, however, because we want to encourage you to love such women, but only so that, if through lack of caution you should be driven to love them, you may know, in brief, what to do.

Robin in this play is not an outlaw, but Marion's sweetheart and a country boy, who is obviously singularly unequal to the knight in status, gallantry and martial prowess, but has nevertheless a spunkiness and jauntiness which makes him an attractive hero. Marion is likewise memorable for her high spirits and loyalty to her lover. The play has a certain number of features which distinguish it as comic entertainment such as the ribald banter of the shepherds, the high jinks involved in the playing of games well known to the court which would have encouraged extempore banter and fun, the doubles-entendres, the music, the singing and dancing and the happy conclusion when Robin and Marion, as lovers crowned in garlands, lead the company in a dance bidding the aristocratic audience and their attendants farewell. Many or all these elements will be ultimately grafted into the English May Games which will be staged not for the French speaking court but for English village society and in the English language. Part of the appeal must surely have been the selection of a hero and heroine from the lower orders of a rigidly hierarchical society who are seen to be brought into dramatic confrontation with authority (against which there was often no redress) and yet, not only do they win out, they remain undaunted and indeed merry. Also part of the interest in this play is in the consideration of the nature of love, then a popular theme in literature.

The following is the first scene of Adam de la Halle's French pastourelle with a translation.

The sections which were set to music in de la Halle's day have been indicated in the text by a ★

Noms de Personnages (Characters)

Robins	Huars
Marions ou Marote	Li Rois
Li Chevaliers	Warniers
Gautiers	Guios
Baudons	Rogaus
Peronelle ou Perrete	

CHI COMMENCE	HERE BEGINS

LI GIEUS	**THE GAME**
DE ROBINS ET DE	**OF ROBIN AND MARION**
MARIONS	

C'ADANS FIST	BY ADAM
ALIAS	or

LI JEUS DU BERGIER ET	THE GAME OF THE
DE LA BERGERE	SHEPHERD & SHEPHERDESS

MARIONS   **MARION**

*Robins m'aime, Robins m'a;	* Robin loves me, Robin is mine
Robins m'a demandée, si m'ara.	Robin wants me, he shall have me.
Robins m'aca cotele	Robin has bought for me
D'escarlate bonne et bele	a fine scarlet dress,
Souskanie et chainturele,	a petticoat and belt,
A leur i va!	*A leur i va !*
Robins m'aime, Robins m'a;	Robin loves me, Robin is mine,
Robins m'a demandé. Si m'ara.	Robin wants me, he shall have me.

LI CHEVALIERS   **KNIGHT**

*Je me repairoie du tournoiement	*I am returning from tournament
Si trouvai Marote seulete	And I find Marion alone
Au cors gent.	The girl with the gorgeous body.

MARIONS   **MARION**

He! Robins, se tu m'aimes,	Oh Robin, if you love me,
Par amors maine-m'ent	Save me, for love's sake!

LI CHEVALIERS   **KNIGHT**

Bergiere, Diex vous doinst	God give you good day,
bon jour !	Shepherdess !

MARIONS   **MARION**

Diex vous gart, sire !	God keep you, sir!

LI CHEVALIERS
Par amor,
Douche puchele, or me contés
Pour coi ceste canchon cantés
Si volontiers et si souvent ?
Hé Robin, si tu ma'aimes,
Par amours m'aime-m'ent

MARIONS
Biaus sire, il a bien pour coi:
J'aim bien Robinet, et il moi ;

Et bien m'a moustré qui'il m'a chiere
Donné m'a ceste panetiere,

Ceste houlete et cest coutel.

LI CHEVALIER
Di-moi, véis-tu nul oisel
Voler par deseure ces cans ?

MARIONS
Sire, j'en ai veu sai kans;

Encore I a en ces buissons

Cardonnereuls et pincons
Qui mout cantent joliment

LI CHEVALIERS
Si m'aït Dieus, bele au cors gent

Che n'est point che je demant ;

Mais véis-tu par chi devant,
Vers ceste riviere, nul ane ?

MARIONS
C'est une beste qui recane;
J'en vi ieer .iij. Sur che quemin,
Tous quarchiés, aler au molin:
Est-che chouque vous demandés ?

LI CHEVALIERS
Or sui-je mout bien assenés !
Di-moi, véis-tu nul hairon ?

KNIGHT
Sweet girl, tell me now
For love's sake, for whom
Are you continually and merrily
Singing the song that goes
Oh Robin, if you love me
Save me, for love's sake ?

MARION
Good sir, it's obvious —
I love Robby dearly, and he loves me ;

He has shown well that he holds me dear
For he has given me this little basket

This crook and this knife

KNIGHT
Tell me, have you seen any birds
Flying about these fields?

MARION
Sir, I've seen I don't know how many.

There are still some in those bushes,

Goldfinches and finches,
All singing gaily.

KNIGHT
God give me strength, you lovely creature,
That wasn't exactly what I was asking ;
Have you seen perchance a duck
Round here, making its way towards the river ?

MARION
Is that some kind of braying beast?
I saw three yesterday, all laden,
en route for the mill.
Is that what you wanted to know ?

KNIGHT
I'm not getting very far, here.
Tell me, have you seen a heron ?

MARIONS

Hairons ! Sire, par ma foi ! Non,
Je n'en vi nesun puis quaresme
Je n'en vi mengier chiés dame
Eme,
Me taiien, cui sont ches brebis.

LI CHEVALIERS.

Par foi ! Or sui-jou esbaubis,
N'ainc mais je fus si gabés.

MARIONS

Sire, foi que vous mi devés !
Quele beste est-che seur vo
main?

LI CHEVALIERS

C'est uns faucons.

MARIONS

Mengüe-il pain ?

LI CHEVALIER

Non, mais bon char.

MARIONS

Cele beste?

LI CHEVALIERS

Esgar ! Ele a de cuir le teste.

MARIONS

Et où alés-vous ?

LI CHEVALIERS

En riviere

MARIONS

Robins n'est pas de tel maniere,
En lui a trop plus de deduit:
A no vile esmuet tout le bruit
Quant ile joue de se musete

LI CHEVALIERS

Or dites, douche bregerete,
Ameriés-vous un chevalier ?

MARIONS

Biaus sire, traiiés — vous arrier.
Je ne sai que chevalier sont;
Desueer tous les homes du mont
Je n'aimeroie que Robins.
Chi ivient au vespre et au matin,
A moi, toudis et par usage;

MARION

Herring ! Sir, by my faith, no!
I've not seen any since Lent
When we ate them at my
grandmother's, Dame Emma's.
These are her sheep.

KNIGHT

I'm struck dumb. To be sure
I've never been so muddled .

MARION

Sir, as you owe me some courtesy
What kind of beast is that on your
wrist ?

KNIGHT

It is a falcon.

MARION

Does it eat bread ?

KNIGHT

No, only good meat.

MARION

What, a beast like that !

KNIGHT

Take a look! It has a leather head !

MARION

And where are you going?

KNIGHT

Down by the stream.

MARION

Robin's not like his sort,
He's much more merry:
He stirs up our whole town
When he plays his bagpipes.

KNIGHT

Now tell me, sweet shepherdess,
Could you love a nobleman ?

MARION

Back off, fine sir.
I don't know any noblemen ;
Of all the men in the world,
I only love Robin.
It's his custom to seek me out here
Every day, evening and morning ;

Chi m'aporte de son froumage:
Encore en ai-je en mon sain,

Et une grant pieche de pain
Que il m'aporta a prangiere.

LI CHEVALIERS
Or me dites, douche bregiere,

Vaurié-vous venir avœc moi

Jeuer suer che bel palefroi,
Selonc che bosket en che val ?

MARIONS au Chevaliers
*Aimi! Sire, ostés vo cheval,
A poi qui il ne m'a blechie.
Li Robins ne reiete mie
Quant je vois après se karue
LI CHEVALIERS
Bregiere, devenés ma drue
Et faites che je vous proi
MARIONS au Chevalier
Sire, traiiés ensus de moi
Chi estre point ne vous affiert
A poi vos chevaus ne me fiert.
Comment vous apele-on ?
LI CHEVALIERS
Aubert.
MARION
*Vous perdés vo paine, sire
Aubert,
Je n'amerai autrui que Robert.

LI CHEVALIER
Nenni, bergère ?
MARION
Nenni, par ma foi.
LI CHEVALIERS
Cuideeriés empirier de moi ?

To bring me some of his cheese.
(I've got some of it left in my bodice
As well as a big hunk of bread)
Which he brought me at dinner time.

KNIGHT
Well now, tell me pretty shepherdess,
How would you like to come with me
On this lovely palfrey
And play games
Down by that thicket
In the valley ?

MARION to the Knight
* Oh dear! Sir, back off your horse
It nearly kicked me.
Robin's horse doesn't lash out
When I walk behind the plough.
KNIGHT
Shepherdess, be my love
Please grant my request.
MARION to the Knight
Sir, keep away from me:
It's not seemly for you to be here.
I was very nearly kicked by your horse
What is your name ?
KNIGHT
Aubert.
MARION
* You are wasting your time, Sir Aubert,
I shall never love anyone except Robin
KNIGHT
No-one, shepherdess ?
MARION
No-one, truly !
KNIGHT
Do you think that you will be de meaned by An association with me ?

Chevaliers sui, et vous bregiere,

Qui si lonc jetés me proiere
MARIONS au Chevalier
Jà pour che ne vous amerai.
 *Bergeronnete sui;
Mais j'ai ami...
Bel et cointe et gai

LI CHEVALIERS
Bregiere, Diex vous en doinst
joie!
Puis qu'ensi est, g'irai me voie.

Hui mais ne vous sonnerai mot.

MARIONS au Chevalier
*Trairi, deluriau, deluriau,
deluriele, Trairi, deluriau,
deluriau, delurot.

LI CHEVALIERS
*Hui, main jou chevauchoie
Lés l'oriere d'un bois;
Trouvai gentil bregiere,

Tant bele, ne vit roys.
Hê! Trairi, deluriau, deluriau,
deluriele,
Trairi, deluriau, deluriau, delurot

I am a knight, you a mere
shepherdess,
Refusing to answer my prayer
MARION to the KNIGHT
I could never love you just for that.
*I am a little shepherdess;
But I have a lover
Handsome, well-mannered and
merry.

KNIGHT
Shepherdess, God give you joy of
him!
Since this is so, I shall go on my
way.
From this moment on, I shan't say
another word to you.

MARION to the Knight
*Trairi, deluriau, deluriau,
deluriele, Trairi, deluriau,
delurau, delurot.*

KNIGHT
This morning I was riding
By the edge of a wood
When I came across a pretty
shepherdess,
(A king had never seen lovelier).
Well I say! *Trairi, deluriau, deluriau,
deluriele,
Trairi, deluriau, deluriau, delurot.*

3 Robin Hood and Maid Marion, and the May Games

> Honour to bold Robin Hood,
> Sleeping in the underwood !
> Honour to maid Marian,
> And to all the Sherwood clan !
> Though their days have hurried by
> *John Keats, Robin Hood*

The Spring Festival and the month of May were sacred to the various manifestations of the Earth Mother. In Scandinavia the 'Lady' was wheeled through the fields in Spring; her consort was called the 'Lord'. Later she was called Freyja and her male attendant Freyr (these titles also mean lord and lady).

Other cultures had corresponding figures whose names meant lord and lady and in England the lord and lady presided over the May Games and still survive as a 'King' and a 'Lady' in the Peak District in the Castleton Garland celebrations on Oak Apple Day and in the characters associated with the Winster Morris Dance.

On the Continent the vacuum created by Christianity with regard to a female deity led to the cult of the Blessed Virgin Mary and the dedication of the month of May and the pagan May festivities to her. The mother of the Virgin, St Anne, was created from a Celtic goddess Anu. Mary thus became Marianne (Mary the daughter of Anne) and the Marianne cult developed with the Marianne figure as an alternative to the Lady or May Queen. In the church calendar in western Europe, the Pentecost holidays became the favourite time for dramatic entertainments featuring the descendants of the Summer Lord and Lady. In France, as we have seen, May and Whitsun games featured a shepherdess called Marion and her lover Robin drawn from the Pastourelles.

9   Friar Tuck and Maid Marian dance at the end of The Play of Robin
Hood and Friar Tuck
*(Tonbridge Mummers' performance at Anne of Cleve House, Lewes for Sussex
Archaeological Society) (photo Fran Doel)*

In England and Scotland the figures of Robin and Marion (or
Marian as her name was often spelt in England) merged with the
outlaw traditions and Robin Hood and Maid Marian became
interchangeable with the Lord and Lady of the May Games from at
least the fifteenth to the early seventeenth centuries in many market
towns, until the games were banned by the Puritans.

The activities are variously called the 'revels' or 'sport' of Robin
Hood at Croscombe, 'the May play called Robin Hood' at Reading
and in other areas games, ales, pageants, dances and gatherings. The
games in Scotland were usually on Sundays in May — the Scottish
poet Alexander Scot mentions:

> In May quhen men zeid everichone
> With Robene Hoid and Littill Johne
> To bring in bowis and birkin bobbynis.

But in England Whitsun was the favourite time and sometimes the
'May' was in June and the name may well denote the blooming of the
hawthorn (brought in to the towns as part of the festivities) rather than

10   *The May Queen ceremonies at Robin Hood's Bay 1901*

the month. A Bedfordshire churchwarden's account refers to 'the May which was the 10 of June 1565' and William Warner wrote:

> At Paske began our morris, and ere Pentecost our May,
> Tho Robin Hood, Li'ell John, Friar Tuck and Marian deftly play.

The plays could extend over a period — the Prior of Worcester for example gave gifts to performers of Robin Hood plays between Whit week and the end of July.

David Wiles in his *The Early Plays of Robin Hood* and Ronald Hutton in his *The Rise and Fall of Merry England* have researched much valuable detailed information on Robin Hood and the May Games. Ronald Hutton mentions that the May Games in England (under various names) are recorded in 104 parishes between 1450 and 1550, (the majority of parishes for which information survives), in 24 of which Robin Hood replaces or joins the 'King' as the central character. Both Ronald Hutton and David Wiles stress the geographical locations of the Midlands, South and West (eg Wells, Croscombe, Exeter, Chagford and Cornwall), with concentrations in the Thames and Severn valleys. Though the North of England has few recorded May Games, and none featuring Robin Hood, David Wiles points out the popularity of both in Scotland (eg Edinburgh, Perth and Aberdeen).

David Wiles' examination of The Church-warden's Account Book from Kingston-upon-Thames provides much valuable information on the interface of May Games with Robin Hood and his outlaws, though the first reference he has traced is a payment of 20d to certain players who performed the *Play of Robin Hood* before the Mayor of Exeter in 1427.

The churchwardens were involved in organising the local May Games, which included collections for poor relief and church repairs. The figure of the Summer Lord and/or Robin Hood, was often used as a focal point for the collecting. Expenses paid to those playing the role of Robin Hood and his band (often including Little John, Friar Tuck and Maid Marian), are listed in the accounts.

Churchwardens' accounts at Reading list Robin Hood plays from 1498 until 1507. The churchwardens at Reading received 19s for the 'gadering of Robin Hood' in 1499 and in 1501 sixpence was paid 'to minstrels at the choosing of Robin Hood'. The morris is subsequently mentioned and so is Maid Marian. At Thame Whitsun ales are listed from the mid fifteenth century, with three references to money being gathered by Robin Hood, the last being in 1501. In the 1550s a 'Summer Lord' did the collecting at Thame, supported by morris dancers in green coats. There does seem to be a degree of interchangeability and continuity in all this, with perhaps the terminology being flexible for similar events. At Amersham in 1530 money is received 'of the lord for Robin Hood'. At Henley-on-Thames the Robin Hood game and the 'king-game' appear interchangeable for the last decade of the fifteenth century and the first decade of the sixteenth century, and there is reference to a Robin Hood of Henley visiting the Reading King game in 1505. The Summer Lord at Melton Mowbray had a sheaf of arrows in 1546 and the Melton accounts of 1556 mention twenty nine shillings and sixpence 'received of Stephen Shaw that he gathered and his company at Robin Hod's play two years'. David Wiles's conclusion on examining his evidence is that 'There is good reason for believing that the Robin Hood game is a version of the king game, and that Robin Hood is a variant of the May King or Summer Lord.'

The Kingston-Upon-Thames accounts of chamberlain and churchwardens from 1507-36 for Mayday contain charges for Robin Hood, Little John, Maid Marian and Friar Tuck. In 1509 they paid 12s 10d for a piece of Kendal cloth to make coats for Robin and John, 3s for three yards of white cloth for Friar Tuck's habit, 3s 4d for four yards of Kendal cloth for Maid Marian's hooded cloak, 4d for gloves for Robin and Marian and 6d for six broad arrows. Payment was also provided for refreshments for the performers, including 2s 8d for two kilderkins of three-halfpenny beer. The gathering at Kingston in 1506 received 39s 10d 'received of Robin Hood's gathering from Whitsunday unto Fair Day at night' and in 1509 4 marks 20d 'received at the Kingham and for the gathering of Robin Hood.' Contributors were given liveries or pins. In 1506 the Kingston wardens paid 4s 2d to John Painter for 1,000 liveries, 3s 8d to William Plott for 1,200 liveries and 40 large ones, and 10d to William Plott for 2,500 pins. So large numbers of spectators/contributors were involved.

Accounts from Reading record similar payments for costumes in 1501, 1503, and 1505, and payments for liveries and pins in 1501; receipts from the 'gathering' are recorded in 1498, 1503 and 1507. In 1509 at Kingston, Maid Marian was paid 2s 'for her labour for two years'. The Reading accounts record visits from Robin Hood and his Company both from Henley and Finchampstead, where Robin's activities involved Morris dancers and minstrels. When the Wednesbury Robin Hood and his band were accused of riotous assembly at Willenhall in 1497 whilst making a gathering, their defence was customary right, that, as in days of yore Robin had come with the Abbot of Marham 'to gather money with their disports to the profit of the churches'.

Henry Machyn saw Robin Hood, Little John, Friar Tuck and Maid Marian in the London May Games of June 1559. As late as 1566 churchwardens at Abingworth paid one and sixpence 'for the setting up of Robin Hood's bower'. The sixteenth-century *Play of Robyne Hode and Fryer Tucke* begins with an announcement that it is 'verye proper to be played in Maye games'. Doubtless many of the quarterstaff combats recounted in the ballads originated in the May Games.

The Tudor chronicler Hall gives two accounts which connect Henry VIII with Robin Hood revelry and which show, that at least by the early sixteenth century, the aristocracy were paying attention to the Robin legends and his connection with Summer celebrations:

> [Soon after Henry's coronation he] came to Westminster, with the quene, and all their traine: and on a tyme being there, his grace, the erles of Essex, Wilshire, and other noble menne, to the numbre of twelve, came sodainly in a morning into the quenes chambre, all appareled in short cotes of Kentish Kendal, with hodes on their heddes, and hosen of the same, every one of them his bowe outlawes, or 'Robyn' Hodes men; whereof the quene, the ladies, and al other there, were abashed, as well for the straunge sight, as also for their sodain commyng: and after certayn daunces and pastime made thei departed.

11   The Town Crier Introduces the 'Hal-an-Tow' at Helston

Hall also describes Henry VIII and Queen Catherine of Aragon going Maying and being 'captured' by 'Robin Hood' in 1516:

> The King and the quene, accompanied with many lords and ladies, roade to the high grounde on Shooters hill to take the open ayre, and as they passed by the way they espied a company of tall yeomen, clothed all in grene, with grene hoods and bowes and arrowes, to the number of two hundred. Then one of them whiche called hymselfe Robyn Hood, came to the kyng, desyring hym to see his men shote, and the kyng was content. Then he whistled, and all the two hundred archers shot and losed at once; and then he whisteled again,and they likewyse shot againe; their arrows whisteled by craft of the head, so that the noyes was straunge and great, and muche pleased the kyng, the queen, and all the company. All these archers were of the kynges garde, and had thus appareled

themselves to make solace to the kynge. Then Robyn Hood desyred the kyng and quene to come into the grene wood, and to see how the outlawes lyve. The king demaunded of the quened and her ladyes, if they durst adventure to go into the wood with so many outlawes. Then the quene said, if it pleased hym, she was content. Then the hornes blewe tyll they came to the wood under Shooters Hill, and there was an arber made of bowes, with a hall, and a great-chamber, and an inner chamber, very well made and covered with floures and swete herbes, whiche the kyng muche praised. Then said Robyn Hood, Sir, oulaws' breakfast is venison, and therefore you must be content with such fare as we use. Then the kyng and the quene sate doune, and were served with venison and wine by Robyn Hood and his men, to their great contentacion. Then the kyng departed and his company, and Robyn Hood and his men them conducted; and as they were returnyng, there met with them two ladyes in a ryche chariot drawen with five horses, and every horse had his name on his head, and on every horse sat a lady with her name written....and in the chayre sate the lady May, accompanied with lady Flora, richly appareled; and they saluted the kynge with diverse goodly songs, and so brought hym to Grenewyche. At this maiying was a greate number of people to beholde, to their great solace and comfort.
(quoted by Joseph Ritson in *Robin Hood*)

From the early sixteenth century we find an interaction between the Morris Dance and Robin Hood plays. The Morris Dance was a male only ritual dance, but there was often a man dressed up as a woman and or a Fool and sometimes a Hobby Horse attendant on the dancers. References indicate that the Marian and other figures representing the Lady were at least sometimes played by men. It is very possible that male Marians were the rule, just as women's parts were taken by men and boys on the Elizabethan and Jacobean stage. In Shakespeare's *The Two Gentlemen of Verona* , the heroine Julia (who would have been played by a boy actor) is disguised as a boy and says:

for at Pentecost,
When all our pageants of delight were play'd,
Our youth got me to play the woman's part,
And I was trimm'd in Madam Julia's gown.
(IV iv 156-9)

At Kingston, six pairs of shoes for Morris Dancers in the May Games are mentioned as an expense in the accounts as early as 1510. In 1536 they had coats of fustian and bells on their garters — eight pairs — for the six dancers, the fool and the 'mowrem' (possibly a male Maid Marian). Thomas Nashe, the Elizabethan pamphleteer describes a male Maid Marian:

> Martin himself is the Maid Marian, trimly dressed up in a cast gown and a kercher of Dame Lawson's, his face handsomely muffled with a diaper-napkin to cover his beard, and a great nosegay in his hands

As the sixteenth century progressed, both civic and ecclesiastical authorities became increasingly uneasy about collecting funds for church repairs and poor relief in the boisterous fashion of the May Games. Bishop Latimer was outraged to find a church where he wanted to preach locked on a holiday, because the citizens were 'gone to gather for Robin Hood':

> I sent word overnight into the town that I would preach there in the morning because it was a holiday ... and when I came there the church door was fast locked. I tarried there half an hour and more. At last the key was found, and one of the parish comes to me and says, 'Sir, this is a busy day with us, we cannot hear you. It is Robin Hood's day. The parish are gone to gather for Robin Hood. I pray you, let (disturb) them not.'
>
> ... It is no laughing matter, my friends, it is a weeping matter, a heavy matter, a heavy matter under the pretence of gathering for Robin Hood, a traitor and a thief, to put out a preacher, to have his office less esteemed — to prefer Robin Hood before the ministration of God's word.
> (Sermon of 1549 by Bishop Latimer, referring to an incident between 1535 and 1539)

It was in Scotland that the May Games were first banned, by statute at Ayr in 1555:

> In all times coming no manner of person be chosen Robert Hood nor Little John, Abbot of Unreason, Queens of May, nor otherwise, neither in borough nor to landward in any time to come.

This reference seems to show that Marian and Tuck are interchangeable with the Queen of May and the Abbot of Unreason (or any other local comic mock-ecclesiastic).

By 1561 Robin Hood was becoming a subversive symbol. Rioting Edinburgh craftsmen and apprentices in that year consorted 'efter the auld wikit maner of Robene Hude' and elected a tailor as Robin Hood, calling him 'Lord of Inobedience'. But it is from Scotland that we find one of the last records of a May Game at Linton in the Cheviots in April 1610. The play featured a Robin Hood, a Little John, a Sheriff and an Abbot of Unreason and all four actors were fined and excommunicated.

There is an interesting survival of Robin Hood's connection with the May Games in the celebration of the 'Hal-an-Tow' which precedes the famous Furry Dance May festival at Helston in Cornwall. Traditionally the 'Hal-an-Tow' song was sung as people went into the woods to gather greenery early on May morning and again as they entered the town to decorate it with their vegetation. The first verse of the song is:

> Robin Hood and Little John
> They both are gone to Fair, O
> And we will go to the merry greenwood
> To see what they do there, O
> And for to chase, O
> To chase the buck and doe.

This prelude to the Furry Dance celebrations (which may originally have been of great ritualistic significance in its own right) was banned as being too rowdy in the nineteenth century, but revived in 1930. Nowadays Robin Hood and his followers in costume mime out the actions to the song in eight or so early morning venues in Helston. Unfortunately there is no trace of Robin Hood at that other great Cornish May festival survival at Padstow.

The Victorians re-introduced a number of May ceremonies, usually with young girls as May Queens and no sexual partners. The Reverend R Jermyn Cooper, for instance, revived May ceremonies at Robin Hood's Bay on the Yorkshire coast in 1862, with a May Queen and maypole, but no Robin Hood or Summer King.

4 The Robin Hood folk plays

For I am Robyn Hode, chief governour under the green-wood
(Ballad of *Robin Hood and the Potter*)

The churchwardens' accounts and other evidence strongly suggest dramatic performances involving Robin Hood and his band at the May Games; and there are also texts which survive. The earliest is a fragment of forty two lines from about 1475 concerning Robin Hood and the Sheriff. This manuscript is claimed to have been found among the Paston family documents, with household accounts dated from May 1473 to August 1475 on the reverse. The Paston family rose to become East Anglian 'gentry' in the fifteenth century and left a mass of correspondence which makes them an important source for historians.

On the 16 April 1473 Sir John Paston wrote to his brother (also John) from Canterbury complaining that he is short of retainers and that the yeoman Woode, an archer in his employ who should have accompanied him on his trip to France has not been made available to him. Although Wood was, as Sir John acknowledges, partly employed to perform in plays of St George and Robin Hood and the Sheriff of Nottingham, he is now in desperate need of retainers and begs that another servant, Mylsent, be sent speedily to him in Calais:

> W Wood, which promised you and Daubeny, God have his soul at Caistor that if ye would take him in to be again with me, that then he would never go from me. And thereupon I have kepyed him thys 3 yere to pleye Seynte Jorge and Robynhod and the shyrff of Nottingham, and now when I wolde have a god horse he is gon into Bernysdale, and I without a kepere.

The implication here is that Woode was initially engaged not just for his keeper's skills but because of his acting ability in performing in the May Games Robin Hood plays and in a St George play (which could either be a Summer play or performed as one of the Midwinter Mummers' plays). The reference to Barnsdale is presumably an ironical joke — the man is unavailable for the journey because of his impending involvement in traditional Robin Hood plays. The date of the letter is highly significant — it is a week before St George's Day, on which a St George's Play was perhaps to be performed at one of The Paston properties. It is also two weeks before May Day, on which Robin Hood plays might be due to be performed, particularly as the text of one turned up amongst the Paston papers.

The reference is crucial in proving the link between retainers and traditional drama and also in support of Professor Holt's theory on the transmission of the stories through the yeoman retainers of the great families. In his next surviving letter (3 June 1473) Sir John is complaining of a lack of a good archer, so it is tempting to conclude that W Woode was a yeoman retainer and keeper, skilled in archery, who therefore took the appropriate part of Robin Hood in local May Games and was well-known for this and combined acting with his other duties. Where did this acting take place? This is harder to establish as the Pastons owned several properties at this time, but the letters were addressed to John Paston in Norwich.

The fragmentary text does not indicate the speakers, but because of the similarity to the ballad *Robin Hood and Guy of Gisborne*, and some references in the text, it is possible to assign names. An unnamed knight (presumably Sir Guy of Gisborne as in the ballad) comes to an agreement with the Sheriff for a bounty for killing Robin Hood. The text jumps straight into the meeting between Robin and Sir Guy and their competition at various sports such as wrestling and throwing stones. The recognition of Robin is omitted, but there are two fights to the death, as in the ballad, and Robin wins:

Sir Guy   Syr sheryffe, for thy sake,
                    Robyn Hode wull I take.

Sheriff   I wyll the gyffe golde and fee,
                    This beheste thou holde me [if you keep this pledge with me]

Sir Guy   Robyn Hode, ffayre and free
                    Undre this lynde shote we.

Robin   With the shot I wyll
                    Alle thy lustes to full-fyll.

12   *Robin Hood and Friar Tuck fight with quarterstaffs from the* Play of
Robin Hood and Friar Tuck.
(Tonbridge Mummers at Plumpton College) (photo Geoff Doel)

Sir Guy	Have at the pryke! [I shoot at the target]
Robin	And I cleve the styke [And I cleave the wand]
Sir Guy	Let us caste [throw] the stone.
Robin	I graunte well, be Seynt John!
Sir Guy	Let us caste the exaltre.
Robin	Have a foot before the! Syr Knyght, ye have a falle. [You are overthrown]
Sir Guy	And I the, Robyn, qwyte shall; [I shall quit you Robin] Owte on the! I blowe myn horne.
Robin	It ware better be un-borne: [better not to have been born]

Lat us fyght at outtraunce. [let us fight to the uttermost]
He that fleth, God gyfe hym myschaunce!

Robin Now I have the maystry here,
Off I smyte this sory swyre [head]
This knyghtys clothis wolle I were,
And in my hode his hede woll bere.

The text then moves, without any comment, into a conversation between Little John and Will Scarlet who seem first to be travelling towards a conflict involving the Sheriff, secondly to be commenting on Friar Tuck's bowmanship and thirdly to be surrendering to the Sheriff:

Little John Welle mete, felowe myn,
What herst thou of gode Robyn?

Will Scarlet Robyn Hode and his menye
With the sheryffe takyn be.

Little John Sette on foote with gode wyll
And the sheryffe wull we kyll.

Little John Be-holde wele Frere Tuke
Howe he dothe his bowe pluke!

Sheriff Yeld yow, syrs, to the sheryffe,
Or elles shall your bowes clyffe. [be cut]

Little John Now we be bownden alle in same:
Frere Tuk, this is no game.

Sheriff Come thou forth, thou fals outlawe,
Thou shall be hangyde and y-drawe [hung and drawn]

Friar Tuck Now, allas, what shall we doo?
We moste to the prysone goo.

Sheriff Opyn the gatis faste anon,
And late theis thevys ynne gon. [and let these thieves go inside]

(From Professor Child's *English and Scottish Popular Ballads vol 3*)

Although Little John is captured in the ballad *Robin Hood and Guy of Gisborne* (and released by Robin Hood disguised as Sir Guy) there are a number of differences from this second section and the ballad (for instance the allusion to the capture of Robin Hood). Our own Mummers team (*The Tonbridge Mummers*) who perform the other two traditional Robin Hood plays have found this fragment very difficult to stage, even put in a wider context. In particular the variety of the competitions between Robin and Sir Guy demand virtuoso performers with many skills (unless the actions are mimed). However the May Games did involve archery and other competitions and the difficulties of this play perhaps give an insight into the type of physically skilled performers taking part in the Robin Hood plays in the fifteenth and early sixteenth centuries before the Morris Dancers took over the roles of Robin and his outlaws. The plays seem to have had a considerable emphasis on action and spectacle.

The other dramatic Robin Hood material to survive from the May Games are one and a half plays appended by William Copland to his edition of the *Mery Geste of Robyn Hoode*, thought to have been published between 1548 and 1569. Firstly there is a complete play with a similar action to the seventeenth-century ballad (which is thought to be of older origin) of Robin Hood and the Curtal Friar. This is immediately followed, without a division, by part of a play which in action corresponds to the first half of the early ballad *Robin Hood and the Potter*. Bizarrely, Copland proclaims these one and a half plays that have no connection (except in the characterisation) on his title page as 'a newe play for to be played in Maye games very plesaunte and full of pastyme'. He gave the one and a half plays the title of *The Play of Robyn Hoode*. The consensus of opinion is that Copland is using, possibly reworking, two early Tudor Robin Hood May Game plays. The texts are reprinted by Professor Child (omitting the bawdy ending of the first play) in volume 3 of his *English and Scottish Popular Ballads* and, in entirety in Dobson and Taylor's *Rymes of Robyn Hood*.

The first complete play (which for convenience we can call *Robin Hood and Friar Tuck*) begins with a formal announcement (which in our revival for The Tonbridge Mummers we give to an officially dressed presenter):

> Here beginnethe the Playe of Robyn Hoode,
> verye proper to be played in Maye Games.

The action begins with Robin calling together his men:

> Now stand ye forth my mery men all,
> And hark ye what I shall say;

Apart from Robin, only Little John among the outlaws is given a short speaking part, but there would presumably be some other 'outlaws' present (perhaps Will Scarlet and Much the Miller's son and perhaps Allen a' Dale doubling as minstrel). The centrepiece of the play is the long confrontation between Robin Hood and Friar Tuck, in which Robin gives voice to his dislike of friars in general in no uncertain terms:

> Of all the men in the morning thou art the worst,
> To mete with the I have no lust; [I have no wish to meet with you]
> For he that meteth a frere or a fox in the morning,
> To spede ell that day he standeth in jeoperdy. [He is in danger of faring ill that day]
> Therfore I had lever [rather] mete with the devil of hell,
> Fryer, I tell the as I thinke,
> Than mete with a fryer or a fox
> In a mornyng, or I drynke. [before I drink]

The language has a certain dramatic vigour which works well in performance, particularly if re-enforced by gesture (which helps in explaining the archaic words). Even the colloquial phrases added to get the rhyme ('or I drynke') work better in a live performance than being read in a book.

The argument leads to the famous scene of the Friar carrying Robin across a stream and depositing him in the middle:

Friar Tuck   Now am I, frere, within, and, thou, Robin, without,
To lay the here I have no great doubt.
Now art thou, Robyn, without, and I , frere, within,
Lye ther, knave; chose whether thou wilte sinke or swym.

Was the play intended to use an actual stream with Robin Hood falling in? This would of course enormously add to the dramatic excitement, but also to the potential of something going wrong or someone being injured. Again one senses that men of action, able to fight with

13   Friar Tuck's dogs attack Robin Hood's men in The Play of Robin
Hood and Friar Tuck
(The Tonbridge Mummers at Tonbridge Castle). (photo Geoff Doel)

quarterstaff, shoot with bow, and take a tumble in a stream in addition
to some acting and dancing ability were what were required.
Elizabethan actors were of course required to be very versatile (as are
their current equivalents in the Royal Shakespeare Company and at
the Globe). For our modern revivals of the play, we carry with us a
'mock' river and 'ham' the falling in scene up, which can work
surprisingly well and is much easier and safer to stage!

Robin's soaking results in a fight, and we feel sure the Tudor
audiences would have expected a good quality quarterstaff fight. As
usual Robin loses (his skill is in archery) which has comic effect and
he summons his band by blowing his horn:

Friar Tuck   Here be a sorte of ragged knaves com in,
                   Clothed all in Kendal grene

Friar Tuck counteracts by whistling for his pack of dogs. In the ballad
a substantial group of outlaws are overwhelmed by a substantial pack
of dogs, but in the play there are only three dogs and presumably only
three or four outlaws in the scuffle. The three dogs are specifically
referred to earlier in the play, but just before the scuffle the Friar says:

> Now Cut and Bause!
> Breng forth the clubbes and staves,
> And downe with those ragged knaves.

If the attack is by dogs (as in the ballad) the reference to clubs and staves is puzzling. Are 'Cut' and 'Bause' men or dogs? Were trained dogs used (such as Will Kemp's famous dog in Shakespeare's *Two Gentlemen of Verona)* or did men or boys impersonate dogs? Did Friar Tuck lead in actual dogs in the beginning but use men (or men or boys impersonating dogs) for the fight? There is an old adage about never acting with dogs or children, but the Tonbridge Mummers use children volunteers from the audience to impersonate dogs to bring 'downe ... those ragged knaves'.

Robin overcomes the embarrassment of defeat by the usual method of inviting the victor to join the outlaw band and he gives Friar Tuck a 'lady free' and invites him to be her chaplain, or private priest. As the play ends with a dance of the Friar and the lady and the Friar's traditional dancing partner in the May Games was Maid Marian (in latter years at least a male morris dancer disguised as a woman), we must assume she is Maid Marian. Her role here as a shared harlot for the outlaw band could not be further from Anthony Munday's conception of her as Lady Fitwalter on the London stage, but it is perhaps more compatible with her origins as a fertility goddess. So shocked was Professor Child with the sexual explicitness of the Friar's final speech that he excluded it and pretended it didn't exist, and even today audiences are amusedly shocked by the wording:

> Here is an huckle duckle,
> An inch above the buckle.
> She is a trul of trust,
> To serve a frier at his lust,
> A prycker, a prauncer, a terer of sheetes,
> A wagger of ballockes when other men slepes.
> Go home, ye knaves, and lay crabbes in the fyre,
> For my lady and I wil daunce in the myre for veri pure joye.

This perhaps seems more comic and less indecent if the context is a burly bearded morris dancer dressed up as the Marian. Though an elegant and attractive lady Marian can also visually enhance the play. The Tonbridge Mummers have used both male and female Marians in their presentations. Either way the end dance and musical accompaniment need to be of a high standard. Tudor comic drama

14   Friar Tuck and Maid Marian at the conclusion of The Play of Robin Hood and Friar Tuck.
(The Tonbridge Mummers at Plumpton College). (photo Geoff Doel)

(and Shakespearean comedy) tended to end with dance and music to emphasis concord and harmony.

The fragment which immediately follows *The Play of Robin Hood and Friar Tuck* is clearly telling the same story (and perhaps based on) the ballad *Robin Hood and the Potter*. The dramatic action covers the first part of the ballad, where Robin converses with Little John, meets the Potters Lad and then gets into an argument and a fight with the Potter over a right of way:

Potter   Why should I paye passage to thee?

Robin   For I am Robyne Hode, chief governoure
                 Under the grene woode tree.

Potter   This seven yere have I used this way up and downe,
                 Yet payed I passage to no man;
                 Nor now I wyl not beginne, so do the worst thou can.

The audience's sympathy (in the midst of the sixteenth-century enclosure of common land and public rights of way) would undoubtedly have been with the Potter. Robin, the liberal outlaw, is becoming tyrannical. In the ballad, and no doubt in the complete play, the Potter soundly beats Robin, who is rescued by Little John. The story proceeds with Robin exchanging clothes with the Potter and selling his wares at Nottingham Fair and giving some free pots to the Sheriff's wife. He decoys the Sheriff into Sherwood and robs him, but spares him a white palfrey in honour of his wife. All this involves extra scene changes for a fair and a forest as well as extra characters — the Sheriff and his wife — and a palfrey (or perhaps a hobby horse). It may be for these reasons that Copland only decided to print the first half of the play, or perhaps the latter part had been lost or not written down. It seems likely, however, that his original source would have been a play based on the entire story in the ballad.

For the Tonbridge Mummers' performances of *Robin Hood and the Potter* we have restored the second part (based on the action and language of the ballad), we use a small set for Nottingham Fair and either real or mock trees for Sherwood Forest. We begin the play with the singing of part of the ballad and end with a dance featuring Robin and Marian and the Sheriff and his wife.

Robin Hood is also the lead character in a Mummers play collected by Reginald Tiddy from Shipton-Under-Wychwood in the Cotswolds, four miles from Burford. Mummers plays are ritual folk drama with a basic pattern of combat, death and resurrection, usually performed at the Christmas period. It is likely that the combatants in these plays from at least the sixteenth century (if not earlier) were St George and a crusading enemy such as a Turkish Knight. Somehow at Wychwood, Robin Hood and Little John have entered the Christmas play and it is Little John who is killed and revived by Doctor Good. In the Cotswolds there is a tradition of the Morris Dancers taking non-dancing parts in Mummers Plays at Christmas in their local villages and possibly this is how the transference of Robin Hood characters occurred, perhaps involving Morris dancers who took the parts of Robin Hood and Little John in the local May games. There is a specific reference to dancing in the text, unusual in the context of other Mummers plays, when a commonly recorded line from the Doctor is juxtaposed with an original rhyming line and a following couplet not found elsewhere:

> I travelled through England, through Scotland, and France,
> Know me little John lets have a English dance.

15   The Potter fights Robin Hood in the play Robin Hood and the Potter *(Tonbridge Mummers performance at the Kent Museum of Rural Life) (photo Archie Turnbull)*

> Green sleevs and yellow lace,
> Four monkeys dance apace.

We feel that the latter three lines (the latter two of which are shorter in stresses than usual for Mummers plays' rhymed couplets), have been added because of the Morris dance connection. Green with yellow braid or attachments is the most commonly recorded colour for the Summer Lord and or Robin Hood and their followers in the May Games.

The other clue to the development of the play is that the first part corresponds textually to the ballad of *Robin Hood and the Tanner* (or *Robin Hood and Arthur A'Bland*), found in several seventeenth-century collections of broadside ballads. It is another ballad in which Robin is defeated in quarterstaff play and asks the victor to join his band. In the ballad Little John challenges the Tanner, who has defeated Robin, but is prevented from fighting him by Robin. Here the rather muddled text without line divisions or names of speakers suggests that the Tanner kills Little John:

Little John to the Tanner:The (you) must be condemned bold fellow if thou so feat to do if the (you) lookst so stout thee (you) and I'll have a bout and thee shalt tan my hide too.

"Fight little Johns killed" (stage direction)

5   The search for the historical Robin Hood

Mony ane speaks o grass, o grass,
And mony mare o corn,,
And mony ane sings o gude Robin Heed
Kens little whare he was born.

(Ballad: *The Birth of Robin Hood*, from the Kinloch MSS)

The earliest known definite reference to the legendary Robin Hood is by William Langland in his poem *Piers Plowman*, dated circa 1377. Langland personifies the Seven Deadly Sins in his poems, and Sloth enters to make a confession (falling asleep in the middle of it) and says:

> I can noughte perfitly my pater-noster as the prest it syngeth,
> But I can rymes of Robyn Hood and Randolph erle of Chestre,
> Ac neither of owre Lorde ne owre Lady the leste that euere was made.

(I don't know my paternoster perfectly as the priest sings it,/ but I do know rhymes of Robin Hood and Randolph Earl of Chester,/ but not the least that ever was written about our Lord and our Lady.)
(*Piers Plowman* Passus V lines 401-403)

This allusion shows that Robin Hood ballads were widely current by the latter half of the fourteenth century. J.A.W Bennett in the footnotes to his edition of *Piers Plowman* compares this reference bewailing that knowledge of Robin Hood stories is greater than knowledge of religious texts, to an early fifteenth-century reference in *Dives and the Pauper* (c1410), which speaks of those who prefer 'to heryn a tale or a song of robyn hode or of sum ribaudry than to here masse or matyns'. Note that this later reference is to hearing rather than reading. In the *Piers Plowman* reference Sloth knows 'rymes', which are presumably in oral circulation.

Professor Bennett also draws attention to the Tudor work *Godmanys Primer*, which comments: 'it is a shame to se so many prentyses so well learned in Robyn hode and naughty trifels and so fewe that knowe the commaundements of God, their belefe, nor their Pater Noster.'

The *Piers Plowman* reference brackets Robin Hood with an historical outlaw, Randoph Earl of Chester. This is presumably the third Earl, Rannulf de Blundeville (1172-1232). Although no romances or ballads survive about Rannulf, the likely contents of some have been reconstructed in R.M. Wilson's *The Lost Literature of Medieval England*. The stories include a fictional involvement in an attempt to depose King John.

Even in the middle ages there seems to have been considerable doubt as to whether Robin Hood had actually existed. There are two early fifteenth-century references which implies that Robin Hood was not a real person. *The Reply of Friar Daw Topias to Jack Upland* mentions that:

> many men speak of Robyn Hode
> That shotte never in his bowe.

and Hugh Legat's vernacular sermon at St Albans in 1410 says that 'mani ... spekith of Robyn Hood that schotte never in his bowe'.

The similarity of the wording of these two references suggests a contemporary proverb and we can thus infer that even by the time of these early references the origin of Robin Hood was obscure. The wording of the proverb suggests a mythological or folklore origin, but if there is any historical basis to the legend it seems likely to be earlier — perhaps considerably earlier — than the fourteenth century.

There was also doubt in the early fifteenth century as to whether the centre of Robin's activities is Sherwood Forest or Barnsdale, a wild region some forty miles further north in Yorkshire. A marginal scribble in a Lincoln Cathedral manuscript of about 1410 reads: 'Robyn hod in scherewod stod, hodud and huthed and hosut and schod four and thuynti arowus he bar in hit hondus'. In 1429 a Judge in the Court of Common Pleas quoted the phrase: 'Robin Hode in Barnesdale stode'. Both these references sound as if they come from Robin Hood songs or poems and they give alternative spheres of action. *The Gest of Robyn Hode* has: 'Robyn stode in Bernesdale, And lenyd hym to a tre.'

The same rhyme seems to be referred to in a list of members of Parliament in Wiltshire in 1432, where an acrostic (a vertical reading of the surnames) of some of the sureties reads off as 'Robyn hode inne grenewode stode, Godeman was he'.

16   Robin Hood's Well, Barnsdale (photo Geoff Doel)

Fifteenth-century clerks and lawyers certainly had a penchant for witty plays on Robin Hood rhymes. There are further sixteenth-century allusions to the phrase, including *The Interlude of the Four Elements* (c1526), where one of the characters cites 'Robyn Hode in Barnysdale stode', and it also features in the eighteenth century ballad *Robin Hood and Allen A Dale.*

Both Barnsdale and Sherwood were the haunts of outlaws and outlaw bands in the Middle Ages. A follower of Simon de Montfort, Roger Godberd, became a notorious outlaw in Sherwood Forest, in the second half of the thirteenth century, committing robberies and murders over a four year period. A reward of 100 marks was offered by the government to the Constable of Nottingham Castle, Reynold de Grey, for his capture. There is also an early fourteenth-century reference to an armed guard being strengthened by twenty archers 'on account of Barnsdale'. The specific references to local sites in Barnsdale in *The Gest* are tantalising, particularly that of 'the Saylis', which has been identified as Sayle's Plantation on the northern edge of Barnsdale, five hundred yards east of Wentbridge. Dr John Maddicott recently discovered a privy seal warrant of June 1329 recording a robbery at 'le Saylles' by two men of Doncaster and others. A stone of Robin Hood near the Great North Road in Barnsdale is the earliest known Robin Hood place-name reference, whilst the most famous is Robin Hood's Well (now only marked by a splendid well cover designed by Sir John Vanbrugh) which survives in a lay-by on the A1, six milers north of Doncaster. The regions of Sherwood and Barnsdale are also linked by a curious story (cited in Joseph Ritson's *Robin Hood*) of King Richard I pursuing a hart from Sherwood to Barnsdale in 1194 and making a proclamation at Tickhill that the hart should not be pursued, but allowed safely to return to the Forest.

A couple of early fifteenth-century incidents show that Robin and his followers were regarded as archetypal outlaws. A petition to Parliament in 1439 mentions the rescue of a prisoner by a Derbyshire man, Piers Venables, and adds:

> and after that tyme, the same Piers Venables, hauynge no liflode ne sufficeante of goodes, gadered and assembled unto him many misdoers, beyge of his clothing ... and, in manere of insurrection, wente into the wodes in that contre, like as it hadde be Robyn hode and his meyne.

And in Royal writs of 1417 and in a letter of 1429 there are references to a malefactor who called himself 'Frere Tuk', and who had an armed band of outlaws and committed murders and robberies in Sussex and Surrey. He was a chaplain and the adoption of the *non de plume* of Friar Tuck was therefore most appropriate. Professor Holt in his *Robin Hood* suggests that this was the original of the Friar Tuck legends, but we feel that it is much more likely that this clergyman is choosing a well-known and appropriate *non de plume* for his double calling of bandit and clergyman from folk tradition. As we show in this book, the Friar Tuck tradition develops from the May Games and revelling figures such as the Abbot of Unreason and the Abbot of Marham and is likely to be well established by the early fifteenth century.

That the Robin Hood legend is extensively known by this period is shown by evidence in the Aberdeen Manuscript Council Register in 1438 of a ship called the *Robyne hude*. Indeed, the earliest specific references to Robin Hood as an historical personage come strangely enough in three Scottish chronicles — perhaps because of Robin Hood's popularity in the Scottish May Games. Andrew de Wyntoun, writing about 1420, assigns Robin and Little John to the years 1283-85:

> Than litill Johne and Robyne Hude
> Waichmen were commendit gud,

ROBIN HOOD:

A

COLLECTION

Of all the Ancient

POEMS, SONGS, AND BALLADS,

NOW EXTANT,

RELATIVE TO THAT CELEBRATED

English Outlaw:

To which are prefixed

HISTORICAL ANECDOTES OF HIS LIFE.

LONDON:

PRINTED FOR C. STOCKING, 3, PATERNOSTER-ROW,
By J. and C. Adlard, Bartholomew-close.

17   *Frontispiece to Ritson's* Robin Hood *(1795)*

> In Yngilwode and Bernysdale
> And usit this tyme thar travale.

(Then Little John and Robin Hood had a reputation as successful outlaws and at this time operated in Inglewood and Barnsdale.)

About 1440, Walter Bower referred to Robin Hood and Little John under the date of 1266:

> At this time the famous outlaw Robin Hood, together with Little John and their companies, rose to prominence among those who had been disinherited and banished on account of the revolt. These men the stolid commons remember, at times in the gay round of comedy, at others in the more solemn tragic vein, and love besides to sing of their deeds in all kinds of romances, mimes and snatches.

This is the first reference which suggests a political or social grievance which has driven Robin and John to become outlaws and is the beginning of a long written tradition (generally unsupported in folklore and folksong) of Robin as social rebel and freedom fighter culminating in Joseph Ritson's *Life of Robin Hood* and Sir Walter Scott's novel *Ivanhoe* and influencing children's literature of the nineteenth and twentieth centuries in Britain and America and twentieth-century films and television serials. Bower comments on the many dramatic and song versions of the legends performed in his day.

Finally, John Major's *History of Greater Britain* of 1521 places Robin and John against the dates of 1193/94 during the reign of Richard the Lionheart, but when Richard was a prisoner in Austria and England was being ruled by Prince John:

> About the time of King Richard 1, according to my estimate, the famous English robbers Robert Hood and Little John were lurking in their woods, preying only upon the goods of the wealthy. This Robert retained with him a hundred well-armed men, whom a force of 400 would have hesitated to attempt to dislodge. His deeds are sung all over England … he was the prince of robbers, and the most humane. He permitted no harm to women, nor seized the goods of the poor, but helped them generously with what he took from abbots.

The wording of this chronicle suggests doubt about the specific dates of Robin Hood and Little John ('according to my estimate') as if Major is trying to fit them into an historical framework. He sees Robin and John as popular heroes celebrated by folksong (which accords with our knowledge of surviving ballads and May Game plays). Major's account is an early reference to Robin's trait of taking from the rich (here specified as rich abbots) and giving to the poor, which is elaborated in the later Robin Hood traditions, literature, films and television and becomes a hallmark of the outlaw tradition elsewhere, particularly in America (Pretty Boy Floyd) and Australia (Ned Kelly and Ben Hall).

Richard Grafton, a Tudor printer who claimed to have an 'aunciente pamphlet' on the subject of Robin Hood, also assigned him to the reign of Richard the Lionheart. Grafton also mentions Robin Hood's gravestone at Kirklees Abbey (where Robin died and was buried according to *The Little Geste of Robin Hood* and the ballad Robin Hoode his Death). There are several further early references to this gravestone, including William Camden, editor of *Brittania*. The original inscription is said to have been:

Here lie Roberd Hude, William Goldburgh, Thomas

An eighteenth-century owner of Kirklees Priory investigated the ground below the grave-slab and concluded there had been no burial and that the slab had been moved there from another site. The slab was subsequently badly defaced by railway labourers seeking charms to ease toothache, was enclosed in railings and had a spurious inscription added. It remains inaccessible on the private Kirklees estate at the time of writing.

Matthew Parker's *The True Tale of Robin Hood* (1632) gives the date of Robin's death at Kirklees as 1198; the Epitaph is placed at the end of his *Tale*:

The Epitaph which the Prioresse of the Monastery of Kirk Lay in Yorke-shire set over Robbin Hood, which ... was to bee reade within these hundreth yeares, though in old broken English, much to the same sence and meaning.

Decembris quarto die, 1198: anno regni Richardii Primi 9.

Robert Earle of Huntington
Lies under this little stone.
No archer was like him so good:

18   Kirklees Priory Gatehouse, after an etching from Ritson's Robin Hood

His wildnesse named him Robbin Hood.
Full thirteene yeares, and something more,
These northerne parts he vexed sore.
Such out-laws as he and his men
May England never know agen.

Some other superstitious words were in it, which I thought fit
to leave out.

Thomas Gale, dean of York from 1697-1702 records an epitaph from
Robin's grave giving his death as December 1247.

In 1795 Joseph Ritson, A Jacobin and a regular correspondent with
Sir Walter Scott, attempted a biography of Robin Hood. Ritson was
convinced of Robin Hood's historicality, but he accepted too many of
the sources uncritically as factual events. However his book provided
a useful compendium of inaccessible material on Robin and gave a
new impetus to the legends by depicting Robin as a romantic
freedom-fighter. His work influenced the portrayal of Locksley in
Scott's *Ivanhoe* and has indirectly shaped virtually all subsequent
literary and film treatments of the legend and the public perception of
Robin Hood.

Over the years two particularly interesting candidates have been put
forward for the historical Robin Hood. The first candidate was
suggested by Joseph Hunter as early as 1852. Hunter was Assistant
Keeper of Public Records and came from the Sheffield area, and
published his theory in a paper entitled *The Great Hero of the Ancient
Minstrelsy of England: Robin Hood*.

Hunter aimed at as literal an interpretation as possible of the events
in the earliest literary account of Robin's career, the medieval *A Gest of
Robin Hood* (see Chapter 1). He did valuable work in identifying place-
names in the Barnsdale region used in the *Gest* and found
documentary evidence showing that armed guards were used to escort
early fourteenth-century travellers through the area because of
outlaws. For example Hunter shows that in 1306 three important
Scottish ecclesiastical prisoners being sent south had their guard
increased between Pontefract to Tickhill 'propter Barnsdale' (on
account of Barnsdale).

Hunter focused on the fourteenth century as he believed in the link
between Robin and one of the King Edwards posited by the *Gest*. Of
the first three post-Conquest King Edwards, Hunter showed that only
Edward the Second had visited the areas specified in the *Gest*. Edward
the Second visited Yorkshire, Lancashire and Nottingham between

19   Robin Hood's Death. From Pierce Egan's Robin Hood & Little John *(1840)*

April and November 1323.

Hunter also traced a Robert Hood, who was a tenant of the manor of Wakefield, listed in the Court Rolls in 1316 with a wife called Matilda, and property and land at Bitchhill. A subsequent entry of 1358 mentioned 'a tenement on Bitchhill, formerly in the tenure of Robert Hood'. Hunter suggested that this Robert Hood was involved in the 1322 rebellion of Thomas of Lancaster, whose followers were outlawed and their lands confiscated after his defeat at the Battle of Boroughbridge.

To fit in with the events of the *Gest* Robin would now need to be pardoned and to enter the King's service. Incredibly Hunter found a series of payments to a 'Robyn Hood' in the accounts of expenses in the king's household (the *Journal de la Chambre* for the period March - November 1324 which lists him as a 'valete de la chambre') and payments cease at the end of the year. This would fit in roughly with the period of fifteen months during which Robin is in the King's service in the *Gest*.

At first sight this did seem a very attractive theory. Initially the two main problems raised by it were the late dating for the 'historical' Robin Hood of the fourteenth century (which raised all kinds of difficulties) and the over-reliance on specific detailed information from the literary *Gest*. It would be unusual for a medieval poem based on orally-transmitted ballads to be specifically accurate on all details of people, places and dates.

Professor Holt has severely undermined Hunter's ingenious and well-researched theory by showing from an ultra-violet light scan of the records that 'Robyn Hode' received wages on 27 June 1323 and thus was already in Edward's service before he visited Nottingham. Professor Holt also discovered a payment recorded on 22 November 1324: 'To Robyn Hod, formerly one of the porters, because he can no longer work, five shillings as a gift, by command.'

So this is probably not our man. And even if we look at the *Gest* as a factual account, as Hunter did, the church was not allowed to lend money at interest or for speculation during the reigns of the three Edwards, (since the Statute of Mortmain in 1279). In the thirteenth century St Mary's Abbey would not have been allowed to profit from the loan of money from Sir Richard by seizing his lands and therefore the loan from St Mary's Abbey would have to derive from an earlier period, under a different king.

Professor Holt and earlier scholars have however built upon Hunter's research into the Hood family of Wakefield showing that the longstanding relationship between the Hood family (containing several Roberts) and the Manor of Wakefield (close to Barnsdale) which began at least as early as the beginning of the thirteenth century. The prototype of our hero-outlaw could have come from that family and area. And some of the earliest place names such as 'Robin Hood's Stone' (1422), 'Robin Hood's Well', 'Robin Hood's Hill' and 'Robinhood strete close' come from the Wakefield / Barnsdale area.

But 'Hood' is a well attested surname throughout England. There was an inn named 'Robin Hood' ('hostel Robin Hod') in Vintry Ward, London in 1294, apparently named after a London councillor called Robert Hood. The Abott of Cirencester had a servant called Robert Hood who slew Ralph of Cirencester in the Abbot's garden between the years 1213 and 1216 and another Robert Hood was imprisoned for offences in the Forest of Rockingham in the 1350s.

Perhaps the most intriguing candidate of all is a Yorkshireman, but one not so far linked with the Hoods of Wakefield. Back in the 1930s Professor L.V.D. Owen tracked down an historical 'Robert Hood, Fugitive'. The Assizes at York in 1226 were presented with details of 32s 6d for the chatels of Robert Hood, fugitive (referred to the following year under a nickname as 'Hobbehod'). The debt was due to the Liberty of St Peter's, York. The Deputy Sheriff of Yorkshire, Eustace of Lowdham, was responsible for collecting and selling the goods and he subsequently became Sheriff of Nottingham in 1232-3.

Professor Owen's possible identification of this historical outlaw with the Robin Hood of legend has a number of attractive features. Firstly the dating is entirely plausible and so are some of the social features. The candidate is known to be an outlaw and Robin Hood's twin enmities in the *Gest* — towards the ecclesiastical authorities in York and the Sheriff of Nottingham — could be explained by this identification. Admittedly the *Gest* mentions St Mary's Abbey and the historical Robert Hood had fallen foul of the Liberty of St Peters, but this is precisely the kind of detail one would expect to become blurred in orally transmitted legends and ballads based on historical events. Did Robin follow Eustace from Yorkshire to Nottingham to pursue a vendetta against the man who distrained his goods and could this finally explain the ancient and puzzling sharing of sites of the traditional Robin Hood stories between Barnsdale and Sherwood Forest?

Another interesting suggestion about this identification is that 'Hobbehod' may have been involved in the movement led by Sir Robert Thwing in 1231-2 against preferments for foreign clergy. His followers robbed foreign monasteries and sold or gave away their

20   Death of Robin Hood — carving on Castle Green, Nottingham by James Woodford (1949)
(photo Geoff Doel)

corn 'for the benefit of the many'. This identification would thus explain both Robin's hatred of abbots and his renowned habit (in later tradition at least) of giving some of his spoils to the poor.

But there may not be a specific historical Robin Hood, or he may be a compound figure. Or the name could be a nickname (like the use of the word 'hood' for a gangster in America. And, as in the case of Friar Tuck, an historical outlaw might have adopted a name from folklore as an alias.

The discovery by Dr David Crook of a William Robehod, fugitive in Berkshire in 1261-2 opened up a whole new series of possibilities in Robin Hood studies, for to have a Robinhood surname in the south of England suggested that the legend was widespread by that time. In the King's Remembrancer's Memorandum of the Royal Exchequer for 1262, the crown pardoned the prior of Sandleford (Berkshire) the mark which the justices of Berkshire had fined him 'because the same prior had seized the chattels of William Robehod, fugitive without warrant'. Further evidence suggests that William was an outlaw and the son of Robert le Fevre and Dr Crook's fascinating interpretation of this is that a clerk or official had changed his name from 'William, son of Robert Le Fevre' to 'William Robehod' as an appropriate nickname for an outlaw. The ramifications of this for understanding the development of the Robin Hood legend are enormous.

Professor Holt has also drawn attention, in his revised edition of his indispensable *Robin Hood,* to eight occurrences of the surname 'Robinhood' discovered in records in the south-east of England living between 1261 and 1296; five of these seem to be criminals. Professor Holt concludes from this evidence that 'Robinhood' had become a nickname for an outlaw or criminal all over the country by the late thirteenth century; this gives us a very early date for the widespread popularity of the legend. The discovery of a 'Katherine Robynhod', probably the daughter of Robert Hood of the Vintry, alerts us to the possibility of 'Robinhood' being a patronym unconnected with outlawry.

The name Robert or Robin has often been linked with 'robber' in popular parlance (perhaps because of the alliteration). There is a Robert the Robber in *Piers Plowman* and it is perhaps in this direction of word association — both with robbery and with the Greenwood that these wide disseminations of the name 'Robinhood' are leading us.

6   Robin Hood's status

You should think
(if you had any hope of soule's salvation)
First, Prior, that he is of thy flesh and blood
That thou art uncle unto Robin Hood
That by extortion thou didst get his lands:
God and I know how it came into thy hands
(from Anthony Munday, *The Death of the Earl of Huntingdon*)

In the ballads and the May Game plays (ie in the popular tradition) Robin is consistently referred to as a 'yeoman'. The concept of yeoman has changed considerably over the years and in Robin's case probably accords with the Chamber's Dictionary archaic definition of 'gentleman serving in a royal or noble household, ranking between a sergeant and a groom'. Such men (of whom Chaucer was an example) would be well skilled in woodcraft, archery and swordplay. Robin is skilled in the use of both bow and sword, but not in the use of a quarterstaff — the peasant's weapon — and it is significant that he loses all of his quarterstaff fights in the ballads and the plays.

Robin's social status explains the wide dissemination of his stories via the travelling retainers and the minstrels who entertained them in the halls of the nobility. It explains the feudal relationships in the ballads (the liveries etc) and Robin's relationship to the Prioress of Kirklees, who would almost certainly have been of gentle birth. And noblemen and their retainers tended to dislike both the more influential members of the church and the petty local officials such as the sheriff and these are popular butts in the ballads.

A somewhat humbler yeoman retainer (but with recognisable Robin Hood traits) is described by Chaucer in the *General Prologue to the Canterbury Tales*:

And he was clad in cote and hood of grene:
A sheef of pecock-arwes brighte and kene
Under his belt he bar ful thriftily;
Wel coude he dresse his takel yemanly.
His arwes drouped noght with fetheres lowe,
And in his hand he bar a mighty bow.
A not-heed hadde he, with a brown visage.
Of wodecraft wel coude he al the usage.
Upon his arm he bar a gay bracer,
And by his syde a sword and bokeler,
And on that other syde a gay daggere,
Harneised wel, and sharp as point of spere;
A Cristofre on his brest of silver shene.
An horn he bar, the bawdrik was of grene.

There seems no doubt that Robin Hood, whether mythical or historical in origin, was a hero celebrated by the ordinary people. He is consistently portrayed as a 'yeoman' in the early sources; this places him in a slightly elevated social position to the commons, reflected by his poor abilities at wielding the quarterstaff in the May Game *The Play of Robyn Hode*.

Increasingly as the upper classes began to take an interest in Robin, beginning with Henry VIII's official antiquary John Leland, they began to try to find noble antecedents for Robin. Leland's reference to Robin as 'nobilis' is the earliest attempt so far found to elevate Robin's social status.

This tradition was built upon by the Elizabethan playwright Anthony Munday in his plays *The Downfall of Robert Earl of Huntington* and its sequel *The Death of Robert Earl of Huntington* in 1598, in which Robin becomes the heir to the Earldom. Marian becomes the historical Matilda FitzWalter, an heiress of whom King John was said to have been enamoured. John poisons Robin in the second play. To depict Robin and Marian as tragic hero and heroine on the Elizabethan stage required elevation of their social status — only in comedies could you have lower class heroes and heroines in that period.

Anthony Munday (c1560 -1633) was a leading dramatist of the day and known as an experimenter in dramatic technique. He is best known for his *Sir Thoms More* (c1593), for which Shakespeare is thought to have contributed a scene. The framework of *The Downfall of Robert, Earl of Huntington* is very interesting as it uses a device for the whole play which Shakespeare sometimes uses for small parts of a play — that of a play within a play. Thus the poet John Skelton plays the

21   *Robin Hood Slays the Foresters in* Robin Hood's Progress to Nottingham *after an engraving by Bewick in Ritson's* Robin Hood *(1795)*

role of Friar Tuck and Sir John Eltham plays the part of Little John and they sometimes appear in their own persons, debating the play. The Sheriff of Nottingham is at first Robin's steward who turns against him and later becomes Sheriff. Other well-known members of Robin's band who feature are Much the Miller's son and Will Scarlet and Will Scathlock, here two people, but originally one and the same in the legends. King Richard returns at the end of the play, a favourite device of later Robin Hood books.

The play begins with the direction 'Enter Roberte, earle of Huntington, leading Marian etc' and commentary by Skelton:

> This youth that leads yon virgin by the hand,
> As doth the sunne, the morning richly clad,
> Is oure Earle Roberte, or your Robin Hood,
> That in those daies, was Earle of Huntington.
> … For many talk of Robin Hood, that never shot in his bowe,
> But Skelton writes of Robin Hood what he doth truly knowe.

Note the reintroduction of the old proverb that we discussed in the last chapter.

Robin dies by poison in the sequel, due to the machinations of Sir Doncaster, a memory of the Abbess of Kirklees's lover Red Roger of Doncaster who is responsible for Robin's death in *The Gest* and *The Death of Robin Hood* ballads. In his dying speech at the end of the play, Robin requests to be buried at Kirklees, linking up once again with tradition. But though there are allusions to Robin's legendary past in both the plays, they are in essence new creations by Munday; their influence on the legend is the lasting influence of King Richard and the concept of Robin's nobility in later literary and film versions.

Matthew Parker's *True Tale of Robin Hood* (1632) also uses traditions of Robin as dispossessed Earl of Huntington (with the *non de plume* of Robin Hood), but combines these with incidents taken from the *Gest*. His epitaph (referring to Kirklees) reads:

> Robert Earle of Huntington
> Lies under this little stone.
> No archer was like him so good:
> His wildnesse named him Robbin Hood.
> Full thirteene yeares, and something more,
> These northerne parts he vexed sore.
> Such out-laws as he and his men
> May England never know agen.

The Sloane manuscript, an anonymous pamphlet about Robin Hood in the British Library dating from the late sixteenth century, hints at a noble birth (though the manuscript is damaged in this section) and gives Robin's birthplace as Locksley (Loxley in Nottingham) in about 1160. A seventeenth-century antiquarian, Roger Dodsworth, gives details of the 'Robin of Locksley' tradition, which influenced Sir Walter Scott's *Ivanhoe* amongst others:

> Robert Locksley, born in Bradfield parish in Hallamshire wounded his stepfather to death at plough: fled into the woods, and was relieved by his mother till he was discovered. Then he came to Clifton upon Calder, and came acquainted with Littel John, that kept the kine; which said John is buried at Hatherhead (*sic* — should be Hathersage) in Derbyshire, where he hath a fair tomb-stone with an inscription.

Sir Walter Scott partly uses the Locksley tradition for his influential *Ivanhoe*, and both Scott and the 1795 biographer of Robin Hood, Joseph Ritson (who was in regular touch with Sir Walter Scott),

22   Robin Hood's Delight. After an engraving by Bewick from Ritson's
Robin Hood

influence traditions of Robin's higher birth. Yet both Sir Walter Scott and the Jacobin Ritson set Robin Hood as a freedom fighter, against the Normans (rather late in the day) on the part of Sir Walter and in general against injustice by Ritson, writing during the heady days of the French revolution. These two writers lead to the revaluing of Robin Hood by writers of the Romantic Movement (with their love of the Middle Ages), a reference in a poem by Keats for instance, and a novel *Maid Marian* by Thomas Love Peacock.

So Robin Hood moves from yeoman to dispossesed aristocrat to freedom fighter to romantic hero. Then comes the descent (if that is the right word) into the swashbuckling hero of children's literature in Britain and America. From this he is saved by the re-injection of mythical and supernatural elements of Richard Carpenter's television series *Robin of Sherwood* in the 1980s, the folk revival in traditions, drama and song, plus the excellent and exciting historical and mythological scholarship of the 1970s and 1980s into the legends. At the time of writing, Robin's status is that of a complex symbol, his class origins being far less important than his cultural role as a link with nature, as a symbol of authority and humanity outside the control and ethos of recognised political and capitalist frameworks and above all of the vitality of the life force.

7 The Greenwood Myth and Arcady

His Scene is Sherwood: And his Play a Tale
(Ben Jonson, *The Sad Shepherd*)

The name Robin is a diminutive of the Norman name Robert, which means 'fame-bright' and is connected to the Germanic 'Rupert' and Latin 'Robertus'. Those who have visualised Robin Hood as a late Anglo-Saxon freedom fighter will be disappointed to learn that the currency of the name Robert in England seems to derive from Norman and Breton cultural and religious influence in the reign of Edward the Confessor and specifically from the Norman Conquest. Robert Champart, from Rouen, was a close advisor of Edward the Confessor, and successively appointed Bishop of London and Archbishop of Canterbury and Edward had a wealthy French relative Robert FitzWimarc who held lands in England. William the Conqueror`s father was Duke Robert of Normandy.

The name Robin seems to have shared with 'Jack' (Jack Frost, Jack a Lent, Jack in the Green) a certain ubiquitous nature, a type name. Many lovers in medieval songs and poems are called Robin (possibly as we have seem because of the 'pastourelles' association). It is also a popular literary name for a good fellow — Chaucer's Miller and Marlowe's Ostler in *Doctor Faustus* are called Robin. And at some stage in the Middle Ages, it became the affectionate name given to the popular bird 'Erithacus rubecula'. The Robin Red-Breast is a sacrificial bird in European folklore — the ballad/story of *The Death and Burial of Cock Robin* is known from many European languages. The bird is curiously associated with human death in folklore — never as an agent of destruction, but trying to mitigate suffering as with its interaction with Christ on the cross in folklore, where it gets its red breast or in the ballad *Babes in the Wood*, where robins cover the dead babes with leaves to protect the bodies.

23   Robin Hood in the Greenwood from Pierce Egan's Robin Hood & Little John *(1840)*

Curiously the ballad *Robin Hood's Death* also has a ritualistic element, with foreknowledge and ritual 'banning' and a death by bleeding, which is suspiciously close to the ritualistic dismemberment of other European and Asiatic Springtime gods and heroes such as Tammuz, Adonis and Osiris. The cognitive connections between Robin the outlaw and Robin the bird may be coincidental, but the possibilities of a Greenwood myth underlying the later outlaw tradition needs to be examined.

There is indeed a familiar 'Robin' Greenwood spirit, known variously as Robin of the Wood and Robin Goodfellow. Some of the place names in the gazetteer may refer to this Greenwood spirit, rather than the outlaw, but there again, perhaps they are one and the same. An example of such a place-name is 'Robin Wood's Rock', a small dolerite outcrop near Beadnell off the Northumbrian coast, shown on the one inch to the mile ordnance survey maps. It is only visible at low tide, so probably is named after the supernatural spirit Robin. Shakespeare's *A Midsummer Night's Dream* is the first allusion to Robin Goodfellow, but his alternative name of Puck in the play has a much older pedigree, extending back to a Irish Pan-like deity called the Pouka and an Anglo-Saxon spirit the Puck. A pamphlet of 1628 entitled *Robin Goodfellow, his Mad Pranks and Merry Jests*, gives Robin Goodfellow's pedigree as the son of Oberon, King of the Fairies, by a human mother. Robin serves Oberon in *A Midsummer Night's Dream*, and one of the fairies describes him as a 'shrewd and knavish sprite/ Call'd Robin Goodfellow' and describes his activities:

> Are you not he
> That frights the maidens of the villagery,
> Skim milk, and sometimes labour in the quern,
> And bootless make the breathless housewife churn,
> And sometime make the drink to bear no barm,
> Mislead night-wanderers, laughing at their harm?
> Those that Hobgoblin call you, and sweet Puck,
> You do their work, and they shall have good luck.

Puck replies:

> I am that merry wanderer of the night.
> I jest to Oberon, and make him smile
> When I a fat and bean-fed horse beguile,
> Neighing in likeness of a filly foal;
> And sometime lurk I in a gossip's bowl
> In very likeness of a roasted crab,
> And when she drinks, against her lips I bob,
> And on her wither'd dewlap pour the ale.
> The wisest aunt, telling the saddest tale,
> Sometime for the three-foot stool mistaketh me;
> Then slip I from her bum, down topples she,
> And "tailor" cries, and falls into a cough;
> And then the whole quire hold their hips and loffe
> And waxen in their mirth, and neeze, and swear
> A merrier hour was never wasted there.

Shakespeare is undoubtedly drawing extensively from folklore for his description. Katharine Briggs in *A Dictionary of Fairies* mentions Robin Round-cap, of Spaldington Hall, who could be helpful by threshing and doing household chores, but when in a mischievous mood, would put fires out, overturn stools and mix wheat and chaff. It is tempting to think there must be some kind of link between the folklore figure of a Greenwood goblin called Robin and the folklore figure of a Greenwood outlaw called Robin. The outlaw (whether real or fictional) could be choosing an appropriate pseudonym. Robin is sometimes an alliterative name given to outlaws in the Middle Ages (such as 'Robert the Robber' in *Piers Plowman*).

One of the oldest surviving ballads *Robin and Gandeleyn* has a hero who is neither Robin of the Wood nor ostensibly Robin Hood, though he is illegally hunting deer. The ballad is found in the Sloane Manuscript in the British Library, which is thought to date from about 1450. The ballad has seventeen verses, fifteen of which are of four lines each, and two have six lines. The use of occasional six-line verses in ballads is a fairly early feature and adds to the pace of the narration with an effective singer or reciter. The first and last verses have a mysterious refrain: 'Robyn lyth in grene wode bowndyn' (Robin lies bound in the Greenwood). This may be intended as a refrain for all the verses, but unfortunately the ballad is not recorded in the oral tradition. The puzzle is that Robin is killed, not captured and bound in the ballad.

Robin's associate in the ballad is Gandeleyn, a name which conjures up the outlaw Gamelyn from a late mediaeval outlaw tale, once thought to have been a part of Chaucer's *Canterbury Tales*. The ballad of *Robin Hood Newly Revived*, printed in several garland versions in the seventeenth century, has Robin Hood's cousin 'Young Gamwell' as the hero who draws blood from Robin. Once their kinship is established, Gamwell joins the outlaw band. The ballad *Robin Hood and the Pedlar*, well known in oral tradition, tells a similar tale and in the version sung by Mr Verral of Horsham, Sussex in 1906 to Vaughan Williams, the hero is called Gamble Gold 'of the gay green woods'. So perhaps there was a tradition of Gandeleyn joining Robin Hood's outlaw band, and even of being related to its leader.

In *Robin and Gandeleyn*, the associates are 'bowmen gode and hende', who are intent on poaching deer:

> He [they] wentyn to getyn hem fleych [meat, food],
> If God wold it hem sende. [if God would send it to them]

They find fifty fallow deer; Robin shoots one of them and is then himself struck down:

> Robyn bent his joly bowe,
> Ther in set a flo; [arrow]
> The fattest der of alle
> The herte he clef a to [he cleft its heart in two]

Festivities in Sherwood Forest.

24   Festivities in Sherwood Forest from Pierce Egan's Robin Hood & Little
John *(1840)*

> He hadde not the der i-flawe [flayed]
> Ne half out of the hyde,
> There cam a schrewde arwe out of the west,
> That felde Robertes pryde.

If this is Robin Hood, then he meets a completely different death to
his traditional fate at Kirklees Priory. At this moment of tension, the
poet uses the first six-liner as Gandeleyn vows vengeance:

> Gandeleyn lokyd hym est and west,
> By every side:
> Hoo hat myn mayster slayin?
> Ho hat don this dede?
> Xal I neuer out of grene wod go
> Til I se his sydis blede.

Wrennok of Donne has done the deed. If 'Donne' is Doncaster, then
this places the action close to Barnsdale, further evidence of a Robin
Hood connection. The two bowman square, aiming at each others'
hearts. Wrennock shoots first:

> Wrennock schette a ful god schote,
> And he schet not to hye;
> Throw the sanchothis of his bryk;
> It towchyd neyther thye.

Gandeleyn vows a better shot, through 'the myght of our lady' (the favourite oath of Robin Hood):

> Gandeleyn bent his goode bowe,
> And set ther in a flo;
> He schet throw his grene certyl,
> His herte he clef on too. [he cleft his heart in two]

> Now xalt thu neuer yelpe, Wrennok,
> At ale ne at wyn,
> That thu hast slawe goode Robyn,
> And his knaue Gandeleyn.

As can be seen by the masterly choice of the verb 'yelp' in the last quoted verse, this poem or ballad is the work of a fine writer. It is a very haunting, ritualistic piece, which hints at a very diverse and complex Robin Hood tradition even by 1450, making it seem even less likely that the figure of Robin Hood derives solely from one historical person whose story was well known.

Towards the end of the sixteenth century, the concept of Robin Hood, or any outlaw living in the Greenwood away from the corruption of civilisation and the iniquity of justice, takes on an Arcadian aspect in song, poem and play. The rigour and harshness of outdoor life is increasingly overlooked and the superiority and freedom of the outdoor life is stressed. The origins of such sophisticated idealism lay in Greek and Roman mythology and literature and is linked with the aristocracy playing at pastoral life in their plays, songs and poems. It is no coincidence that Robin's symbolic link with Arcady coincides with his increasing identification with the aristocracy.

Arcady was a remote Grecian sheep-farming region, isolated, mountainous and the abode of the primitive fertility god Pan. The Roman poet Virgil used it as a setting for his *Eclogues* in the first century BC. Later Renaissance writers of pastoral poetry, such as Sir Philip Sidney in his *Old Arcadia* in which two princes disguise themselves as a shepherd and an Amazon, follow Virgil in using Arcady as a manifestation of the virtues of a simple rural life in contrast to the sophisticated yet corrupt world of the Court.

In Anglo-Saxon and medieval times there was nothing so dreaded as banishment, but the sixteenth century quest for personal identity and fulfilment made a virtue of necessity and equated the outlaw's punishment with his liberation. A contemporary ballad *Birk and Green Hollen* celebrates the freedom of the banished man:

> Where nought is seen but endless green
> And the blue sky in between
>
> So enough for me, enough for me
> To live at large with liberty.

William Warner, writing in 1586, envies the contentment, justness and even the safety of Robin Hood's existence:

> Those days begot some malcontents, the principal of whom
> A County was, that with a band of yeomanry did roam —
> Brave archers and deliver men, since nor before so good.
> Those took from the rich to give to the poor, and manned Robin Hood —
> Who fed them well and lodged them safe in pleasant caves and bowers,
> Oft saying to his merry men: 'What juster life than ours?'

This reinterpretation of Robin and the Greenwood myth is related to the contemporary notion of equating Robin with the nobility. In Shakespeare's *The Two Gentlemen of Verona* and *As You Like It*, noblemen become outlaws in the Greenwood because of injustice.

In *As You Like It*, the old Duke has been banished by his younger brother and Charles the court wrestler reports:

> They say he is already in the Forest of Arden, and a many merry men with him; and there they live like the old Robin Hood of England. They say many young gentlemen flock to him every day, and fleet the time carelessly as they did in the golden world. (Ii 111-115)

The reference to 'Robin Hood of England' is because the play (like its source Thomas Lodge's pastoral romance *Rosalynde or Euphues' Golden Legacy* (printed 1590) is set in Ardennes in France, though Shakespeare by calling it 'The Forest of Arden' clearly has in mind the forest near

Shakespeare birthplace which provided his mother's maiden name. The allusion to the Golden Age refers to a classical mythological concept of an early ideal time when mankind was free from sin, necessity and worry. The Christian parallel is the Garden of Eden before the Fall of Man.

The outlaws in *The Two Gentlemen of Verona* are less reputable and have committed real crimes, but they seem to be gentlemen and share Robin Hood's courtesy towards women. Speed urges Orlando to join the band as 'it's an honourable kind of thievery.' The outlaws swear by 'the bare scalp of Robin Hood's fat friar'.

In 1635 Ben Jonson began a pastoral romance on the subject of Robin Hood entitled *The Sad Shepherd* or *A Tale of Robin Hood*. Never completed, it was obviously intended to have masque like features, with songs, music, dance and poetry, stunning costumes, elaborate backdrops and lighting.

The cast list describes Robin Hood as 'The Chief Wood-man, Master of the Feast' with Marian as 'His Lady, the Mistris' and the Greenwood band described as 'their Family'. The Shepherds and Shepherdesses invited to the feast, as well as being representative of Arcadia and a natural, uncorrupted life style represent moral qualities or types while the remaining characters include the witch Maudlin and her servant Puck-hairy (also termed Robin Goodfellow, a kind of benevolent prankster as is Puck in *A Midsummer Night's Dream*), represent disrupting and even malign influences inherent in society. The play is full of accepted symbols which by then were an integral part of the Robin Hood legend — the period Spring/Summer with Robin and Marian preparing to preside over a celebratory feast in which a King and Queen will be crowned with flowers, the shrine-like floral bower which will become the focal point of the Greenwood activity, the association of Robin with a well, the feast held deep in the woods, the illegal hunting and killing of the deer, and Robin's concern for and protection of the worthy, in this play represented by the Shepherds and Shepherdesses .The other half of Jonson's play was intended to have been concerned with lost love, with the lost shepherdess finally restored to the bosom of her swain. This is how Jonson began the play.

BEN JONSON'S
SAD SHEPHERD

The Persons of The Play

Robin-hood,	The chiefe Wood-man of the Feast
Marian	His Lady, The Mistris

Their Family

Friar Tuck	The Chaplaine and Steward.
Little John,	Bow-Bearer
Scarlet,	Two brothers, Huntsmen.
Scathlock,	Two brothers, Huntsmen
George a Greene,	Huisher of the Bower.
Much,	Robin-hoods Bailiffe, or Acater.

The Guests Invited

Clarion,	The Rich
Lionell,	The Courteous
Alken,	The Sage Shepherds
Aeglamou	The Sad
Karolin	The Kind
Melifleur	The Sweet
Amie	The Gentle Shepherdesses
Laurie	The Beautifull

The Troubles unexpected

Maudlin,	The Envious: The Witch of Papplewicke.
Douce,	The Proud : Her Daughter
Lorell,	The Rude, A Swine'ard, the Witches son.
Puck-hairy,	Or Robin-Goodfellow, their Hine

The Reconciler.
Reuben, A devout Hermit.

The SCENE is *Sher-wood*.
Consisting of a Landt-shape of Forrest, Hill, Vallies, Cottages, A Castle, A River, Pastures, Heards, Flocks, all full of Countrey simplicity. *Robin-hoods* Bower, his Well, the Witches *Dimble*, The Swine'ards *Oake*, The Hermits *Cell*.

25   *Robin Goodfellow — from an early seventeenth-century woodcut*

THE ARGVMENT

Of the first ACT

Robin-hood, having invited all the Shep'erds and Shep'erdesses of the
Vale of *Be'voir*, to a Feast in the Forrest of *Sherwood*, and trusting to his
Mistris, Maid *Marian*, with her Wood-men, to kill him Venison against
the day : Having left the like charge with Friar *Tuck* his Chaplaine and
Steward, to command the rest of his merry men, to see the Bowre
made ready, and all their things in order for the entertainment;
meeting with his Guests at their entrance into the Wood, welcomes
and conducts them to his Bowre. Where, by the way hee receives the
relation of the sad Shep'ard *Eglamour*, who is faine into a deeper
Melancholy, for the losse of his beloved *Earine*: reported to have beene
drowned in passing over the *Trent,* some days before. They endeavour

in what they can do to comfort him: but his disease having taken so strong root, all is in vaine, and they are forced to leave him. In the meantime, Marian is come from hunting with the Hunts-men, where the Lovers interchangeably expresse their loves. *Robin-hood* enquires if she hunted the Deere at force, and what sport he made, how long hee stood, and what head hee bore : All which is briefly answered with a relation of breaking him up, and the Raven, and her Bone. The suspect had of that Raven to be *Maudlin*, the Witch of *Paple-wick*, whom one of the Hunts-men met i' the morning, at the rowsing of the Deere, and is confirm'd by her being then in *Robin-hood's* Kitchen i' the Chimney- corner, broyling the same bit, which was then thrown to the Raven, at the *Quarry* or Fall of the Deere. *Marian* being gone in, to shew the Deere to some of the Shepherdesses, returnes instantly to the *Scene* discontented, sends away the Venison she had kill'd, to her they call the Witch, quarrels with her Love *Robin-hood,* abuseth him, and his Guests the Shep'erds : and so departs, leaving them all in wonder and perplexitie.

THE PROLOGVE

He that hath feasted you these forty yeares,
And fitted Fables, for your finer eares,
Although at first, he scarce could hit the bore;
Yet you, with patience harkning more and more
At length have growne up to him, and made knowne,
The Working of his Pen is now your owne:
He pray's you would vouchsafe, for your owne sake,
To heare him then once more, but, sit awake.
And though hee now present you with such wooll,
As from mere English flocks his Muse can pull,
He hopes when it is made up into Cloath;
Not the most curious head here will be loath
To weare a Hood of it; it being a Fleece,
To match , or those of Sicily , or Greece,
His Scene is Sherwood: And his Play a Tale
Of Robin -hood's inviting from the Vale
Of Belvoir, all the Shep'ards to a Feast:
Where by the casuall absence of one Guest,
The Mirth is troubled much, and in one Man
As much of sadness shown, as Passion can
The sad young Shep'ard, whom we heere present,
Like his woes Figure, darke and discontent,
For his lost Love; who in the Trent is said

To have miscarried;'lasse! What knows the head
Of a calme River whom the feet have drown'd?
Heare what his sorrowes are; and if they wound
Your gentle brests, so that the End crown all,
Which in the Scope of one dayes chance may fall:
Old Trent will send you more such Tales are these,
And shall grow young againe, as one doth please
(fragment)

ACT 1. Scene I
Aeglamour
Here! she was wont to goe! And here! And here!
Just where those Daisies, Pincks, and Violets grow:
The world may find the Spring by following her:
For other print her aerie steps neere left:
Her treading would not bend a blade of grasse!
Or shake the downie Blow-ball from his stalke!
But like the soft West-wind, she shot along;
And where she went, the Flowers tooke thickest root,
As she had sow'd 'hem with her odorous foot

ACT 1 Scene II

Marian, Tuck. John. Wood-men, &c
Mar.Know you, or can you guesse, my merry men,
What'tis that keepes your Master Robin-hood
So long both from his Marian, and the Wood?
Tuc. Forsooth, Madam, hee will be heere by noone,
And prayes it of your bounty as a boone,
That you by then have kild him Venison some,
To feast his jolly friends who hether come
In threaves to frolick with him, and make cheare;
Here's Little John hath harbord you a Deere
I see by his tackling.   **Io** And a hart of ten,
I trow hee be, Madam, or blame your men
For by his Slot, his Entries, and his Port,
His Frayings, Fewmets, he doth promise sport,
And standing 'fore the Dogs; he beares a head,
Large and well beam'd: with all rights somm'd, and spred.
Mar. Let's rowse hin quickly, and lay on the Hounds.
Io. Scathlock is ready with them on the grounds;

So is his brother Scarlet;: now they'ave found
His Layre, they have him sure within the pound.
Mar. Away then, when my Robin bids a Feast
'Twere sinne in Marian to defraud a Guest.

ACT 1. Scene III
Tuck. George a Greene. Much. Aeglamour
Tuc.And I, the Chaplaine, here am leftt to be
Steward to day and charge you all in fee,
So d'on your Liveries ; see the Bower drest ;
And fit the fine devises for the Feast :
You, George must care to make the Baldrick trim,
And Garland that must crowne, or her, or him;
Whose flock this yeare, hath brought the earliest Lmabe !
Geo. Good Father Tuck, at your Commands I am
To cut the Table out of the greene sword,
Or any other service for my Lord;
To carve the Guests large seats; and these laid in
With turfe (as asoft and smooth as the Moles skin:)
And hang the bulled Nose-gaies 'bove their heads,
The pipers banck, whereon to sit and play;
And a fair Dyall to meete out on the day.
Our Masters Feast shall want no just delights:
His entertainments must have all the rites.
Muc. And I all choise that plenty can send in ;
Bread, wine, acates, Fowle, Feather, Fish or Fin,
For which my Fathers Nets have swept the Trent.
Aeg. And ha' you found her ? **Mu**. Whom? Aeg. My drowned Love.
Earine ! The sweet Earine !
The bright and beautiful Earine!
Have you not heard of my Earin ?
Just by your Fathers Mills (I think I am right)
Are not you Much the Millers Sonne ?   **Mu**. I am.
Aeg. And Baily to brave Robin-hood ? **Mu**. The same
Aeg. Close by your Fathers Mills. Earine
Earine was drown'd! O, my Earine!
(Old Maudlin tells me so, and Douce, her Daughter)
Ha' you swept the River say you ? And not found her ?
Muc. For Foewle, and Fish wee have. **Aeg**. O not for her ?
You're goodly friends ! Right charitable men !
Nay, keepe your waye, and leave me: make your toyes,

Your tales, your poesies, that you talk'd of; all
Your entertainments: you not injure me;
Onely if I may enjoy my Cipresse wreath !
And you will let me weepe ('tis all I aske;)
Till I be turn'd to water, as was she !
And troth what lesse suit can you grant a man ?
Tuc. His Phantasie is hurt, let us now leave him:
The wound is yet too fresh, to admit searching.
Aeg. Searching ? Where should I search ? Or on what track?
Can my slow drop of teares, or this darke shade
About my browes, enough describe her losse !
Earine,O my Earine's loss !
No, no, no; this heart will breake first.
Geo. How will this sad disaster strike the eares
Of bounteous Robin-hood, our gentle Master ?
Mu. How will it marre his mirth, abate his feast;
And strike a horror into every guest!
Aeg. If I could knit whole clouds about my browes
And weepe like Swithen, or those watry signes,
The Kids that rise then, and drowne all the Flocks
Of those rich Shepherds, that did let her drowne !
Those carelesse Shepherds, dwelling in this Vale;
Then I did something or could make old Trent
Drunke with my sorrows, to start out in breaches
To drowne their Herds, their Cattle and their corne,
Breake down their Mils, their Dams, ore-turne their weeres,
And see their houses, and whole lively-hood
Wrought into water, with her, all were good :
I'd kisse the torrent, and those whirles of Trent,
That suck'd her in, my sweet Earine !
When they have cast their body on the shore,
And it comes up as tainted as themselves,
All pale and bloodlesse, I will love it stil,
For all that they can doe, and make 'hem mad,
To see how I will hugge it in mine armes !
And hang upon the lookes, dwell on her eyes:
Feed round about her lips, and eat her kisses !
Suck of her drowned flesh! Aand where's their malice ?
Not all their envious sousing can change that :
But I will study some revenge past this !
Pray you give me leave, for I will study.
Though all the Bels, Pipes, Tabors, Timburines ring

That you can plant about me: I will study

ACT 1 Scene IIII
Robin-hood, Clarion, Melifleur, Lionel, Amie, Alken. Tuck, Servants, with Musick of all sorts.

Rob. Welcome bright Clarion, and sweet Melifleur,
The courteous Lionel, faire Amie; all
My friends and neighbours, to the Jolly Bower
Of Robin-hood, and to the greene-wood Walkes :
Now that the shearing of your sheepe is done,
And the wash'd Flocks are lighted of their wooll.

Despite what seems at first like an inordinately complex plot and a multitude of unfamiliar characters, we must not undervalue the immense contribution that Jonson might have made to the Robin Hood legend had he lived to complete the play. The Sherwood outlaws, genial but anarchic and drawn from the lower orders of society are exactly the sort that Jonson relished for his comedies. The characteristics of the new characters Amie, Melifluer, Douce etc are mostly types and apparent from their names. The Prologue carefully spells out the story before it begins for this is not an old story retold, it is a new story of a great feast in Sherwood to which the shepherds and shepherdesses of Belvoir were invited by Robin Hood and his lady Marian. It is also the tale of how one sad young shepherd was restored to his lost love whom he thought had drowned and of Robin's part in the restoration *The Sad Shepherd* promised to be witty, fast moving, fantastic and colourful but in its incomplete state it was ignored in the seventeenth century. In the eighteenth century the play had a continuator in F.G. Waldron and was produced with some success at the Drury Lane Theatre, London. The nineteenth century, however, chose to ignore it.

8 Robin's outlaw band

Friar Tuck and Little John are riding down together,
With quarter-staff and drinking-can and grey goose feather;
The dead are coming back again; the years are rolled away,
In Sherwood, in Sherwood, about the break of day.
(Alfred Noyes, *Sherwood*)

We have already seen that Maid Marian and Friar Tuck are figures derived from folklore and mythology. Marian ultimately from a Spring/Summer goddess through the Whitsun Pastourelles and May Games. Though not mentioned by name, She appears to be the 'trul of trust' given by Robin to the Friar at the end of the sixteenth century May Games play *Robin Hood and the Friar* — a non-speaking and dancing character, whose part may have been taken by a male Morris dancer. She does not feature in the Gest or any of the early ballads, but she is mentioned in several seventeenth-century broadside ballads and plays a prominent part in one of them — *Robin Hood and Maid Marian* — where she appears disguised as a man and defeats her lover, Robin, in a quarterstaff fight. The ballad is not of great literary merit, but is of interest in being influenced by the late sixteenth-century dramatic tradition which equated Maid Marian with Matilda, daughter of Lord Fitzwater:

A bony fine maid of a noble degree
With a hey down down a down down,
Maid Marian call'd by name,
Did live in the North, of excellent worth,
For shee was a gallant dame.

For favour and face, and beauty most rare,
Queen Helen she did excel;
For Marian then was prais'd of all men
That did in the country dwell.

X. ROBIN HOOD AND THE CURTALL FRYER.

26   Robin Hood & the Curtall Fryer engraving after Bewick from Ritson's
Robin Hood

'Twas neither Rosamund nor Jane Shore
Whose beauty was clear and bright,
That could surpass this country lass
Beloved of lord and knight.

The Earl of Huntingdon, nobly born,
That came of noble blood,
To Marian went, with a good intent,
By the name of Robin Hood.

Friar Tuck is one of the many rubicund and dissolute clergy figures affectionately parodied in the May Games, such as the Abbot of Unreason in Scotland and the Abbot of Marham of Wolverhampton who made a 'gathering' at the time of the Robin Hood of Willenhall's visit in 1497. There are records of a mock Abbot of Exeter in the fourteenth-century Summer celebrations in that city, who captured passers-by and forced people out of their houses:

They held them against their will until they had extorted from them certain sums of money in lieu of a 'sacrifice'. And although they appear to attempt this under veil and colour of a game — or rather, a mockery — yet it is undoubtedly theft inasmuch as money is taken from the unwilling, and by force too.

(translated from the Latin by E.K. Chambers in *The Mediaeval Stage*.)

There was also a mock Abbot of Shrewsbury in a painted cloak in the local May games in the sixteenth century, who was replaced by Robin Hood and his men in the first year of the Catholic Queen Mary's reign. Robin and Little John replaced the Abbot of Bon-accord and his Prior in Aberdeen in 1508 and the Abbot of Na-rent at Edinburgh in 1518.

Friar Tuck is almost certainly the 'Friar' of the May Games play Robin Hood and the Friar mentioned above. The action of the play is very similar to that of the very popular seventeenth-century ballad *Robin Hood and the Curtal Friar*. It is thought that the early versions of the ballad derive from an even earlier version, now lost, which may well go back at least to the date of the play. But the Friar does seem to join the exploits of Robin and his band via the May Games.

In both play and ballad Robin asks the Friar to carry him across the stream and deliberately drops him in. In the ensuing fight, Robin seeks aid from his merry men and the Friar from his dogs. The Friar defeats Robin in quarterstaff combat and the dogs defeat the outlaws and Robin asks the Friar to join the outlaw band, where he is to prove a doughty fighter. It is interesting to note that fighting clergymen are associated with other outlaws (eg Hereward the Wake) and Eustace the Monk was a famous pirate and outlaw after the Norman conquest.

Some of the other personalities in Robin's merry band have early references in the *Gest* and ballads. Little John is particularly linked to Robin from earliest times as his chief friend and supporter in the *Gest*, in ballads, in the May Games and early plays and in the Scottish Chronicles.

There is a prevalent seventeenth- and eighteenth-century tradition that Little John was born and died at Hathersage in the Peak District, that he was buried in the churchyard in a marked grave and that his bow was hanging in Hathersage church, together with some arrows, chain-mail and a green cap. The site of his birth and death was said to be a little cottage (now demolished, but a drawing survives) adjacent to Hathersage churchyard. John is reputed to have returned to die at Hathersage after burying Robin Hood at Kirklees Priory.

27   *Robin Hood and Little John (Roxburghe Ballads c 1660)*

The Ballad of Robin Hood and Little John, which describes how John joins Robin's outlaw band after knocking him in a stream during a quarterstaff fight, gives John's surname as Little, Robin reversing his name for comic effect as he is exceptionally tall. However in the Derbyshire tradition, John is a nailor by trade and his surname is also Nailor. It is interesting that a Colonel Naylor is said to have strung John's old bow at Hathersage and shot a deer with it in 1715. The bow was recorded as being made of spliced yew, 79in long, tipped with horn, weighing 2lb and requiring a pull of 160lbs to draw it. The bow and armour were removed from the church in the middle of the eighteenth century, because of the bad condition of the church. A photograph of the bow survives and it was recorded as being in Scotland in 1980.

Little John's reputed grave was opened in 1784 and a thigh bone 32in long was found. The last occupant of Little John's Cottage, Jenny Shard, was visited by the antiquary, Dr Spencer Hall in 1847. She remembered the thigh-bone being brought into the cottage and being measured on her father's tailoring board. Her father told her that Little John had died in the cottage.

A mid-seventeenth-century manuscript of Elias Ashmole says:

> Little John lyes buried in Hathersage Church yard within 3 miles fro Castleton in High Peake with one Stone set up at his head and another at his Feete, but a large distance betweene them. They say a part of his bow hangs up in the said Church. Neere Grindleford Bridge are Robin Hoods 2 Pricks.

A ballad dealing with this tradition called *Little John's End* was written by William Haines and published in volume two of *The Reliquary*.

Will Scarlet (or Scarlok) and Much the Miller's son are companions of Robin in the early ballads and survive through into nineteenth- and twentieth-century children's editions of the stories and into twentieth-century films and televisations. Will Stutley appears in some early ballads, including a popular broadside concerning his own rescue, first listed in the seventeenth century — *Robin Hood Rescuing Will Stutley*, but he has been totally eclipsed or merged with Will Scarlett in recent versions. Gilbert of the White Hand, second only to Robin in archery skill in the early ballads, has not become universally known.

The minstrel Allen A 'Dale, who seems to be a later addition to the legends, has his own eighteenth century ballad and features in the earlier children's literature, but has slipped out of favour in less romantic recent treatments of the Robin Hood legends. *Robin Hood*

MAID MARIAN AND ROBIN HOOD.

𝕭𝖔𝖔𝖐 𝕴𝕴.

I HAVE HEARD TALK OF ROBYNE HODE,
    HEY DOWN AND HEY DOWN A ;
AND OF BRAVE LITTLE JOHN,
OF FRIAR TUCK AND WILL SCARLET,
LOCKSLEY AND MAID MARION,
    HEY DOWN, DERRY DOWN.

28   Maid Marian and Robin Hood from Pierce Egan's Robin Hood & Little John *(1840) and Allen A Dale* is a romantic ballad in which Allen's betrothed is about to be married to an old knight:

> Yesterday I should have married a maid,
> But she is now from me tane,
> And chosen to be an old knights delight,
> Whereby my poor heart is slain.

Robin intervenes to thwart the old knight and Little John marries the young couple. The absence of Friar Tuck is in interesting and Much becomes 'Nick the Miller's Son'.

No political point about rank is made, merely that the lady should be allowed to 'chuse her own dear'. It is the most romantic of all the Robin Hood ballads.

> And thus having ended this merry wedding,
> The bride lookt as fresh as a queen,
> And so they returnd to the merry green wood,
> Amongst the leaves so green.

Gazetteer of sites connected with Robin Hood

No gazetteer can do full justice to the abundant number of places in England that either carry the name of this legendary Greenwood outlaw or one or other of the various members of his band. His name today is being perpetuated in an increasing number of new roads, streets and public houses while older place names, often centuries old, reflect the one-time popularity of the tales of Robin Hood, and the all important May Games which not only heralded the advent of summer but licensed a rural community to enjoy itself. The May Day association with archery in particular, is reflected in the number of English place-names associating Robin with the word 'butt' (a word found in Middle English and which originally meant a 'mound' and used of natural hills and tumuli before its association with the archery butt). Another Middle English word 'butte' also associated with Robin Hood meant 'a strip of land abutting on boundaries' and indicates a site in which archery butts were set up in the medieval period for the community's obligatory archery practice every Sunday (all other games being discouraged on that day). During the reign of Edward III a statute of 1363 ordered that 'shooting the butts' was compulsory on Sundays and Saints' Days. Another statute of 1465 during the reign of Edward IV ordered that all butts should be maintained at the expense of every township and used on Sundays and Feast Days. The targets were often white 'clouts' set up at a distance of about two hundred yards or the 'popinjay' might be used, a painted representation of a bird set up on a stick. The English longbow was of yew, roughly five feet long and had an effective range of two hundred and fifty yards. Robin's brilliance as an archer is relevant whatever his social status as the bow was used by all classes including kings.

29   Robin Wood's Rock, near Beadnell, Northumberland (photo Geoff Doel)

THE BORDERS

Robin Hood's Bog
Northumberland NZ 079261
A stretch of bog land within the enclosed six hundred acre wooded Chillingham Park in which live the famous white cattle, descendants of prehistoric wild oxen.

Robin Wood's Rock
Northumberland NU 236273
A tiny dolerite islet a few hundred yards offshore from Beadnell Bay, visible at low tide

YORKSHIRE

Barnsdale Bar
Yorks SE 511136
Location where the great north road divided. A notorious place for robberies in the Middle Ages and a site for the opening of the Geste.

The earliest recorded Robin Hood place-name , the 'Stone of Robert Hood' recorded in a deed of 1422, was somewhere in the area of Barnsdale Bar.

Robin Hood's Bay
N Yorks NZ 9505

Pantile roofed fishing village a few miles south of Whitby set picturesquely within a ravine. A local story has it that Robin came here to acquire boats to help him escape to Europe. An alternative legend says that Robin shot his bow across the bay, from Stoupe Brow on the south, and resolved to build a town where the arrow fell. The first mention of this name came in Leland's description of the town about 1538 as 'a fischer tounlet of twenty bootes caullid **Robyn Huddes Bay**, a dok or bosom of a mile yn length.'

In 1540 it is mentioned as being part of Whitby Abbey lands.

30   Robin Hood's Bay from the North

31   One of Robin Hood's Butts, North York Moors (photo Geoff Doel)

Robin Hoods Butts

N Yorks NZ 963018

Three tumuli south of the beacon at Stoupe Brow. One tumulus used to be known as Robin Howe (pronounced Hoo in dialect)

Kirklees Abbey

4 miles NE of Huddersfield SE 1742215

Reputed burial place of Robin Hood. When he was dying, Robin took refuge here and shot two arrows from the window of his cell. One fell into the river Calder, the other into the priory and marked the place of his grave. The supposed grave slab which lies about seven hundred yards from the nunnery gate, was said to have been damaged at the time of the building of the Lancashire and Yorkshire railway The gravestone was first recorded in 1584 and a drawing of it made in 1665 including a partial inscription 'Here lie Robard Hude , William Goldsburgh, Thomas…'.

Alternative traditions give the manner of Robin death. A Chap-book version tells us that a treacherous monk bled him to death:-

> This deadly danger to prevent
> He hy'd him with all speed
> Unto a nunnery with intent
> For health's sake there to bleed

34 Robin Hood's Tower, City Walls of York (photo Geoff Doel)

A faithless friar did pretend
In love to let him blood,
But he by falsehood wrought the end
Of famous Robin Hood.

The second legend ascribes his death to the Prioress of Kirklees, Dame Elizabeth, who was his kinswoman. She feigned kindness and bled her sick cousin (bleeding, leeching and cupping were traditional medieval treatments for all 'morbid' humours that caused diseases) but bandaged his arm so loosely that he bled to death during the night. Kirklees was once a Cistercian nunnery, founded in the reign of Henry II with a double dedication to the Virgin Mary and St James and all that survives today is the restored gatehouse. The Prioress's body was said to have been buried within the Priory chapel. (see Chapter 5).

Robin Hood and Little John's Closes (Fields)

Near Whitby NW 918096

Two fields situated a mile and a half south east of Whitby Abbey. In each field is a granite standing stone, 4ft high and about 2ft in diameter. The stones are inscribed 'Robin Hood' and 'Little John' and are known as **Robin Hood's Pillars**. According to an account of 1771 the pillars mark the result of an archery competition between the two after they had dined with the Abbot of Whitby. Little John's arrows outstripped his master's by one hundred feet.

Robin Hood's Howl

West of Kirkbymoorside SE 682869

A natural declevity on the southern edge of the North York Moors.

Robin Hood's Tower

York SE 602524

The northern angle tower of the Walls between Bootham Bar and Monk Bar is referred to by this name in the early seventeenth century.

Robin Hood's Well

Yorks SE 518120

Situated to the east of the A1(M) near Wentbridge, north of Doncaster. It boasts a splendid well cover which was designed by Vanbrugh. The name goes back to at least 1622 and the well was a stopping place for coaches in the eighteenth century. Thomas Gent's 'History of York' describes how 'passengers from the coach frequently drink of the fair water and give their charity to two people.who attend there'.

LANCASHIRE

Robin Hood

5 miles north west of Wigan SD 521115

Tiny hamlet

Robin Hood's Cross

6 miles NW Wigan SD 519141

Ancient cross sited near Mawdesley village

Robin Hood's Bed

5 miles NE of Rochdale SD 975165

An alternative name for Blackstone Edge, a Pennine outcrop north of Rochdale

32   Robin Hood's Pillar and Robin Hood's Field, near Whitby (photo Geoff Doel)

33   Little John's Pillar and Little John's Field, near Whitby (photo Geoff Doel)

WHITBY ABBEY N. W.

35   Whitby Abbey from Whitby: Its Abbey *by F K Robinson (1860)*

THE MIDLANDS

Blidworth
Notts SK 567567
Home of Maid Marian according to nineteen-century tradition. Her birthplace is said to be where Ashfield cottage now stands, opposite the Black Bull. Will Scarlet is said to be buried in the parish churchyard.

Friar Tuck's Cell
Notts SK 567568
Friar's Tuck's cell at Copmanhurst is said to be at Fountain Dale, one and a half miles north west of Blidworth

Friar Tuck's Well
Notts SK 568569
Local tradition says that when the Friar was turned out of his cell the spring dried up for seven years

Edwinstowe
Notts SK 674673
Here Robin and Marion were 'married at the church door' as was traditional at that period, in the twelfth century church of St Mary. The village lies beside common land and on the edge of Sherwood Forest.

36   Edwinstowe Church - legendary site of Robin and Marian's wedding. (photo Geoff Doel)

Little John's Grave, Hathersage (see Chapter 8)
Derbyshire SK 234893
In tradition Little John was both born in and buried at Hathersage. His alledged birthplace was an old cottage next to the Church, now destroyed. His grave is first recorded in sventeenth century and is well looked after today in the churchyard, 7 foot long, between two headstones. A bow said to be his, used to hang in the church it is now thought to be in a Scottish castle.

Loxley
Notts SK 3011900
Joseph Ritson in his *Life of Robin Hood* claims that Robin was born here in Loxley 1160. He deduces this from the Sloane manuscript which says 'Robin Hood was borne at Lockesley ... in the days of Henry the 2nd about the yeare 1160.' The Sloane manuscript is dated to the late sixteenth century Sir Walter Scott calls Robin Hood Robin of Locksley in his novel *Ivanhoe*

37   Little John's Grave, Hathersage Church in the Peak District. (photo Fran Doel)

and there was a tradition recorded in 1637 that the foundations of the house in which Robin was born were visible in Little Haggas Croft.

Nottingham,
Notts SK 5654

Nottingham Castle was seized by Prince John when Richard Lionheart was on his crusade but was forced to surrender the castle to his brother when Richard returned to England briefly in 1194. After becoming king in 1199 John spent a great deal of time here and extensively re-fortified the castle. Inside the Council House is a clock with a bell, named Little John.

The Nottingham Story and The Tales of Robin Hood in the city currently both deal with the Robin Hood Legends.

Papplewick
7 miles due north of Nottingham SK 565652

Alllen a Dale was married here.

Robin Hood's Bed
5 miles NE Rochdale SD 975165

Part of the ridge called Blackstone Edge in the Pennines

Robin Hood's Cave
Derbyshire North of Hathersage SK 244836
A fissure within the crags of Stanage Edge

Robin Hood's Chair
Derbyshire Hope Dale SK 213820
Mentioned in one of the Child ballads Vol 111, 47.

Robin Hood's Cross
The Peak District SK 188302
A very early reference of 1319 refers to *Robins Crosse*. This is earlier than any early place name recorded for Robin Hood but may refer to a proto-type supernatural denizen such as Robin Goodfellow or simply commemorating a person called Robin .In the context of the Robin Hood tradition, its close proximity (three miles to the west) is intriguing.

Robin Hood's Moss
11 miles NW Sheffield SK 190930
Part of moorland in the High peak.

Robin Hood's Picking Rods
Near Glossop SK 008909
Two stone pillars, possibly marking boundaries.

Robin Hood's Pot, Oxton,
Notts. SK 635532
Bronze age round barrow situated outside the west entrance of a hill fort. The barrow is six metres high and twenty seven and a half metres in diameter. Medieval burials were located nearby.

Robin Hood's Stride
SK 223623
Pinnacles twenty two yards apart near Cratcliff Tor on Hartle Moor, three miles south of Bakewell.

Robin Hood's Well (or St Anne's Well)
Nottingham
Referred to as **Robynhode Well** in 1500, **Robyn Wood's Well** 1548 and **Seynt Anne Well** 1551 and **Robyn Hood Well alias Seynt Anne Well** in 1596. The well lies two miles to the NE of the city centre. John Throudy in 1797 desribed the Well "under an arched

*38   Statue of Robin Hood on Castle Green, Nottingham by James Woodford
(1949) (photo Geoff Doel)*

stone roof of rude workmanship, the water is very old, it will kill a toad. It is used by those who are iffiicted with rheunitic pains". He describes a nearby house which displayed relics of Robin Hood, such as his helmet and chair.

Sherwood Forest

Notts, N of the city

The forest which was the reputed greenwood home of Robin and his outlaw band in the medieval period would have extended over 100,000 acres. Today only a few tracts of pasture and forest survive and the area has become a county park A number of trees of great antiquity have acquired folklore associations with Robin Hood. A great oak known as *Robin Hood's Larder* survived until a few years ago and was reputedly the tree on which the outlaws suspended their illegally killed king's venison. A short walk from Sherwood Forest Centre brings one to the famous *Major Oak* where, eighteenth-century accounts tell us, the outlaws were accustomed to gather. The oak was named after an eighteenth-century army officer, Major Rooke. The forest was a royal hunting park which most of the medieval English kings (including Richard Lionheart) used for hunting. A whole host of sites connected with Robin Hood arose in the eighteenth and nineteenth centuries including *Robin Hood's Meadow, Robin Hood'es Cave, Robin Hood's Stable and Robin Hood's Hill*. Much or not all of the folklore with Robin Hood and Sherwood seems relatively recent.

THE SOUTH AND SOUTH-EAST

Robin Hoods Arbour

Maidenhead , Berks SU 852811

Prehistoric earthwork shaped like a square known as Robin Hood's Bower in the seventeenth century.

Robin Hoods Butts

Nr Godalming, Surrey SU 970478

Two hills The antiquarian John Aubrey referred to them under this title in the seventeenth century and they are now known as Bud Burrow and Row Bury.

Robinhood Walk and Robinhood Gate

Richmond Park, Surrey TQ 213723

This great park was created and enclosed in the reign of Charles 1 for

39   The Major Oak, Sherwood Forest (photo Geoff Doel)

royal hunting. It has been suggested that the Robin Hood associations (**'Robinhood Walk'**, **'Robinhood Gate'** etc) date back to the reign of Henry VIII and are an indication of the king's patronage of the May Games. There were a cluster of other Robin Hood place name associations for instance Robinhood Farm

THE WEST & THE WELSH BORDERS

Robin Hood Ball
South of Marlborough, Wilts SU 144474
Neolithic Tumulus

Robin Hood Barrow
Nr Bournemouth, Hants SZ 070931
Tumulus now in woodland (Talbot Woods)

Robin Hood's Bower
Dorset SY
Single round barrow near Puddletown

40   The May Queen, Nancy Storm, with her Maids of Honour at Robin Hood's Bay, First of May 1914. Nancy's speech said that 'May was kept by the early English to commemorate Robin Hood, for it was on May first that he died'. This hints at a lost tradition of Robin's death

Robin Hood's Bower
South of Warminster ST 876424
Circular earthwork

Robin Hood's Butts
Dorset ST 094105
Two round barrows near a public footpath running through a forestry plantation on Pistle Down three miles north of Verwood. Nineteenth-century reference: 'the tumuli in this neighbourhood are called by the peasantry Robin Hood's Butts.'

Robin Hoods Butts
NW Hereford SO 430515
Two small hills three miles east of Weobley

Robin Hood's Butts
Som. South of Taunton ST 230144
Three long barrows near Otterford

Robin Hood's Butts
Som. South of Taunton ST 237128
Five long barrows on Brown Down

The Hal-An-Tow processes through Helston 1992. Maid Marian and Friar Tuck are in the foreground. (Photo Geoff Doel)

Bibliography

Briggs, Katharine, *A Dictionary of Fairies*, Penguin

Bronso, Bertrand, *The Singing Tradition of Child's Popular Ballads*, Princeton

Chambers, E K, *The Mediaeval Stage*

Chaucer, Geoffrey, *The Canterbury Tales (The General Prologue)* Penguin Classics

Child,Francis, *The English & Scottish Popular Ballads (vol 3)*, Dover

Dobson, R B, & Taylor, J, *Rymes of Robyn Hood*, Alan Sutton

Doel, Fran & Geoff, Lloyd, Terry, *Worlds of Arthur*, Tempus

Doel, Geoff & Fran, Deane, Tony, *Spring & Summer Customs in Sussex, Kent & Surrey*, Meresborough

Egan, Pierce, *Robin Hood and Little John, or the Merry Men of Sherwood Forest,* W S Johnson & co

James, Gairdner, Ed *The Paston Letters*, Alan Sutton

Firth Green, Richard, 'The Ballad and the Middle Ages' (from *The Long Fifteenth Century*, a collection of essays edited by Helen Cooper and Sally Mapstone, Clarendon

Grinsell, Leslie, *The Folklore of Prehistoric Sites*

Higham, N J, *The Death of Anglo-Saxon England*, Alan Sutton

Hill, Christopher, *Liberty Against the Law*, Penguin

Hole, Christina, *English Folk Heroes*, Batsford

Holt, J C, *Robin Hood*, Thames & Hudson

Hutton, Ronald, *The Rise and Fall of Merry England*, Oxford

Jonson, Ben, The Sad Shepherd (in vol 3 of *Collected Works* ed by C Herford & Percy and Evelyn Simpson), Oxford

Keen, Maurice, *The Outlaws of Medieval England*, London

Kennedy, Peter, *Folksongs of Britain and Ireland*, Oak Publications

Langland, William, *Piers Plowman*, Clarendon (ed J Bennett)

Lloyd, A L & Williams, R Vaughan*The Penguin Book of English Folksong*

Munday, Anthony, *The Death of Robert Earl of Huntingdon*, Malone Society Reprint

Percy, Bishop, *Reliques of English Poetry,* Swan. Sonnenschein & Co

Reaney, P H, *The Origin of English Place Names*, Routledge & Kegan Paul

Richards, Will, *Friar Tuck and Blidworth Forest*, (booklet — no publishing details in it)

Ritson, Joseph, *Life of Robin Hood*, E P Publishing

Scott, Sir Walter, *Ivanhoe,* Penguin

Shakespeare, William, *The Two Gentlemen of Verona,* Arden

Shakespeare, William, *A Midsummer Night's Dream,* Arden

Shakespeare, William, *As You Like It,* Arden

Sidney, Sir Philip, *The Old Arcadia,* Worlds Classics

Tiddy, Reginald, *The Mummers Play,* Clarenden

Wiles, David, *The Early Plays of Robin Hood*, D S Brewer

Wilson, R M, *The Lost Literature of Medieval England*, Methuen

Robin Hood Filmography

Compiled by Isobel Doel, Steven Morley & Thomas Doel

The first black and white silent films on the Greenwood hero in the 1920s employ debased legendary material depicting Robin as the Earl of Huntingdon, a deposed nobleman in exile, and the swashbuckling leader of a band of outlaws living in Sherwood Forest. Maid Marian is his chaste companion and true love. A superlative bowman, Robin is unfailingly courteous to his enemies and all oppressed righteous men. Also, like the knights of romance and the Robin of the ballads, he shows kindness and respect to women. Although driven into a life of crime, he robs the rich, invariably represented as corrupt churchmen or aristocrats, uniquely to give to the poor and needy. In this he is joined by good hearted and loyal Englishmen, outlaws like himself, who love their country and the absentee king (Richard Lionheart) but hate the oppression and the evil natures of King John and the Sheriff of Nottingham,the villains of the legend. The films also pick up on what was present in the earliest ballads, that Robin is a rebel against authority ,with a particular hatred of the Sheriff of Nottingham, the principal agent of the government of the day and that he and his men are dedicated to the ideal of liberty and the rights of the common people.

The legend of Robin and Marian proved irresistible for Hollywood. The most notable film about Robin in the twenties (on one of the biggest sets ever conceived with Douglas Fairbanks initially protesting that he had no wish to 'play a flat-footed Englishman') was followed by another classic action-packed film in the late thirties with Errol Flynn as Robin of Sherwood Forest. The MGM *Adventures of Robin Hood* made some use of the traditional ballads and stories; Robin was brave and arrogant and knocked into the river by Little John in a quarterstaff fight. Friar Tuck was a brave gourmet and the ballad character of Guy of Gisbourne was excellently developed by Basil Rathbone into the villanous side-kick for Claude Rain's effete Prince John. And so was established a film genre, with every generation bringing out ever afterwards a screen interpretation of Robin Hood and his Merry Men as a projection of the popular imagination of the day.

Robin Hood
(Etienne Arnaud ,Herbert Blache, USA, 1912) b/w, silent
Robert Frazer stars in this early film.
Robin Hood
(Lloyd Lonergan, USA, 1913) b/w, silent
William Russell stars.

Robin Hood
(Allan Dwan, USA, 1922) 127 minutes, silent, b/w
Hero of the silent screen Douglas Fairbanks stars in this, the first big-budget outing for Robin Hood. Lavish sets and epic pageant provide an impressive setting for the sword action.

The Adventures of Robin Hood
(Michael Curtiz, William Keighley, USA, 1938) 105 minutes
The classic Robin Hood film. Errol Flynn in sequined costume and Basil Rathbone star in this swashbuckling adventure, featuring lavish sets and brilliantly choreographed swordfights.

The Bandit of Sherwood Forest
(George Sherman, Henry Levin, USA, 1946) 92 minutes
Splendid-looking romp with Cornel Wilde, let down by a poor script.

Rogues of Sherwood Forest
(Gordon Douglas, USA, 1950) 79 minutes
The son of Robin Hood (John Derek) helps force the signing of the Magna Carta in this bizarre reworking.

Tales of Robin Hood
(James Tinling, USA, 1951) b/w
Enjoyable but noticeably low budget sword-fighting adventure starring Robert Clarke.

The Story of Robin Hood and His Merrie Men
(Ken Annakin, USA, 1952)
Cheery and colourful Walt Disney version of the Robin Hood story starring Richard Todd.

Men of Sherwood Forest
(Val Guest, UK, 1954)
Don Taylor stars as the cavalier hero in another swashbuckling adventure.

Sword of Sherwood Forest
(Terence Fisher, UK, 1960) 80 minutes
Continuation of the Robin Hood saga as the Earl of Newark plans to assassinate the Archbishop of Canterbury. Richard Greene as Robin Hood must save the day.

Robin and the Seven Hoods
(Gordon Douglas, USA, 1964) 123 minutes
Comedy musical where the Robin Hood legend is transported to 1928 Chicago. Frank Sinatra stars as the gang leader Robbo.

A Challenge for Robin Hood
(C.M. Pennington-Richards, UK, 1967) 85 minutes
Barrie Ingham leads this uninspired Hammer Films adventure.

Robin Hood
(Wolfgang Reitherman, USA, 1973) 83 minutes
Animated Walt Disney comedy-musical.

Robin and Marian
(Richard Lester, USA, 1976) 107 minutes
An ageing Robin Hood returns to Sherwood after the Crusades, and must again face the Sheriff of Nottingham. Romantic adventure continuation exploring the theme of heroism, starring Sean Connery and Audrey Hepburn.

Time Bandits
(Terry Gilliam, UK, 1981) 116 minutes
Python-esque fantasy-comedy. Amongst other adventures, time-travelling dwarves encounter John Cleese as Robin Hood with his warped band of Merrie Men.

The Zany Adventures of Robin Hood
(Ray Austin, USA, 1984) 100 minutes
Offbeat comedy parody, featuring George Segal as a beleaguered Robin Hood coping with a bunch of moronic Merrie Men.

Robin Hood
(John Irvin, UK, 1990) 104 minutes
Patrick Bergin stars in a standard but enjoyable retelling of the legend.

Robin Hood: Prince of Thieves
(Kevin Reynolds, USA, 1991) 143 minutes
Glossy blockbuster starring Kevin Costner. Returning from the Crusades, Robin must face the Sheriff (a wicked Alan Rickman) with the help of his Moor companion Azeem and the initially distrustful outlaws of Sherwood Forest.

Robin Hood: Men In Tights
(Mel Brooks, USA, 1993) 104 minutes
Robin Hood spoof, parodying adventure films in general and *Robin Hood: Prince of Thieves* in particular.

Television
The earliest televisations of the Robin Hood legend, such as the series starring Richard Greene in the fifties, were based on children's Robin Hood books of the nineteenth and twentieth centuries. These were ultimately derived from Pierce Egan's *Robin Hood and Little John* (1840), and Howard Pyle's *The Merry Adventures of Robin Hood* (1883), both of which draw on the traditional ballads. The episodic nature of the ballads was ideally suited to a series of half hour adventure stories on television.

Richard Carpenter's Robin of Sherwood was a very popular and influential television series of the 1980s which also extensively used traditional characteristics and stories, but re-introduced a mythical and supernatural element into the stories. This gave them added depth and power, and brought them out of the realm of 'Boy's Own' adventure yarns. Carpenter fused the legends with another greenwood myth, the story of Herne the Hunter, first recorded by Shakespeare in *The Merry Wives of Windsor*. He explained the protean nature of the legends by having several Robin Hoods, all 'sons of Herne'. Carpenter followed the characterisation of Guy of Gisbourne in the Eroll Flynn film, but made him the side-kick of the sheriff. He also introduced a saracen into the outlaw band — copied by the scriptwriters of *Robin Hood Prince of Thieves*, who apparently thought this was a traditional motif! Carpenter's treatment of Little John, Will and Much was both sympathetically traditional and realistic, and Marian successfully combined romantic heroine with liberated modern woman.

Contemporary with this was a humorous and feminist television treatment — *Maid Marian and Her Merry Men*, in which Robin was a wimp and Marian the real brains and courage behind the outlaw band!

Acknowledgements and notes

1   The Robin Hood Ballads & the outlaw tradition
The discussion in this chapter draws on extensive examination of ballads in many collections over a number of years, plus recordings of songs and listening to live performances. In particular we should like to acknowledge the use of Professor Child *English and Scottish Popular Ballads* (especially volume 3); Professor Bronson *The Singing Tradition of Child's Popular Ballads*; Bishop Percy *Reliques of Ancient English Poetry* and Professor Dobson and J Taylor *Rimes of Robyn Hood*.

2   The Pastourelles
Martin, *Le Jeu de Robin et de Marion*
Monsignor, *Li Gieus de Robin et de Marion*.

3   Robin Hood and Maid Marian and the May Games
Cambers, E K: *The Mediaeval Stage*
Wiles, David: *The Early Plays of Robin Hood*
Hutton, Ronald: *The Rise & Fall of Merry England*
Ritson, Joseph *Robin Hood*
Doel, Geoff & Fran, and Deane, Tony, *Summer Customs in Sussex, Kent & Surrey*
The references to the Helston 'Hal-an-Tow' are from our own observations of the custom on several occasions, with words of the song (plus early references to the custom) from Peter Kennedy's *Folksongs of Britain and Ireland*.

4   The Robin Hood folk plays
ed Gairdner, James *The Paston Letters*
Child *The English and Scottish Popular Ballads vol 3*
Dobson & Taylor: *Rymes of Robyn Hood*
Tiddy: *The Mummers Play*

5   The search for the historical Robin Hood
This chapter is particulary indebted to Professor Holt, *Robin Hood*, but also uses Professor Bennett's edition of Langland's *Piers Plowman*,

Ritson: *Life of Robin Hood* & Wilson: *The Lost Literature of Mediaeval England.*

6   Robin Hood's status
The numerous sources include — for the mediaeval and ballad concept of Robin as yeoman:
Professor Child, *The English and Scottish Popular Ballads*
Professor Holt, *Robin Hood*
Ritson, *Robin Hood*
Scott, Sir Walter, *Ivanhoe*
Chaucer's portrait of the Knight's Yeoman in *The General Prologue to the Canterbury Tales*. For the aristocratic Robin Hood, Anthony Munday's two Elizabethan Robin Hood plays reprinted by The Malone Society and Mathew Parker's *A True Tale of Robin Hood* (which is reprinted by Ritson, Child and (in part) by Dobson and Taylor) are especially useful.

7   The Greenwood Myth and Arcady
For our analysis of the woodland spirit Robin of the Wood or Robin Goodfellow, we have drawn on:
Shakespeare, William, *A Midsummer Night's Dream*
Briggs, Katharine, *Dictionary of Fairies* and a range of folklore and sites. For the *Robyn and Gandeleyn* ballad we have used the text in Child's *English and Scottish Popular Ballads* volume 3 (number 115), though our analysis is original. The Arcadian sections draw on:
Sidney, Sir Philip, *The Old Arcadia*
Shakespeare, William, *Two Gentlemen of Verona* and *As You Like It*
Jonson, Ben, *The Sad Shepherd* (available in his *Collected Works*).

8   Robin's Outlaw Band
The ballads in this chapter are quoted from:
Professor Child, *English and Scottish Popular Ballads* volume 3.
The references from the May Games are drawn from a number of sources including Chambers, Wiles and Hutton. Information on Little John comes from a range of Derbyshire traditions.

Gazetteer
We are particulary indebted to the following sources:
Taylor & Dobson, *Rymes of Robyn Hood*;
Holt, *Robin Hood*
Reaney: *The Origin of English Place Names*
Richards, Will: *Friar Tuck & Blidworth Forest*
Grinsell, Leslie: *The Folklore of Prehistoric Sites*

Index